ONDORI
ELEGANT CROCHET LACES

BY YOKO SUZUKI

CONTENTS

Hote : All pieces in this book are worked from stitch symbols rather than from row by row directions. The symbols are explained on pages 101—103.

★Copyright © 1983 ONDORISHA PUBLISHERS, LTD. All rights reserved.
★Published by ONDORISHA PUBLISHERS, LTD., 32 Nishigoken-cho, Shinjuku-ku, Tokyo 162, Japan
★First Edition—1983
★Sole Overseas Distributors : Japan Publications Trading Co., Ltd.,
  P. O. Box 5030 Tokyo, International, Tokyo, Japan
★Distributed in the United States by Kodansha International／U.S.A, Ltd.
  through Harper & Row, Publishers, Inc., 10 East 53rd Street, New York, New York 10022.
ISBN 0—87040—528—4
Printed in Japan

THE FRESHNESS OF WHITE LACE

Ruffled Doily 36cm in diameter
Instructions on page 41

(Opposite page) Leaf-shaped Table Center 77cm by 44cm
Instructions on page 45

Table Center 39cm in diameter
Instructions on page 48

(Opposite page) Table Center 52cm by 32cm
Instructions on page 44

Square Doily 29cm square
Instructions on page 49

ROMANTIC LACE FOR SUMMER

Filet Mesh Table Runner 124cm by 43cm   Instructions on page 49

Rose Tablecloth 133cm square   Instructions on page 52

Rose Pillows 56cm square   Instructions on page 51

Heart-shaped Pillows 53cm by 50cm   Instructions on page 54

Scalloped Collar 6.5cm wide   Instructions on page 58

Mesh Collar 10cm wide   Instructions on page 56

13

Doll Pochette   *Instructions on page 58*

Lace-trimmed Pochette *Instructions on page 61*

16   *Piano Cover Crocheted area 23cm wide Instructions on page 62*

LOVELY DOILIES

You may have many happy memories while you work for these doilies.

They are small in size, but they are gorgeous,

neat and clean. Make hearty gifts to give.

Daisy Doily (Below) 32cm in diameter   Instructions on page 64
Sunflower Doily (Opposite page) 30cm in diameter   Instructions on page 66

Shown below is Breughel Lace Doily, which is made of long braid.

Pineapple patterns are worked inside of curved braid.

Ruffled mesh pattern gives this beautiful Rose Doily more charm.

Breughel Lace Doily (Above) 43cm by 30cm   Instructions on page 67
Rose Doily (Opposite page) 31cm in diameter   Instructions on page 69

Hand-made lace doily reflects your good taste.

It also makes your room look neat and clean.

The color of white lace is changed into ècru or blue

by the sunlight in the morning, noon and evening.

Doily (Above) 32cm in diameter   Instructions on page 66
Doily (Opposite page) 29cm in diameter   Instructions on page 70

The word "Doily" used to mean "Doilnapkin"

which was placed under a finger bowl or a vase.

Make attractive doilies and place them wherever you like.

Doily (Above) 35cm in diameter   Instructions on page 70
Doily (Opposite page) 31.5cm in diameter   Instructions on page 72

WINDOW DECORATIONS

Decorate windows with lace.
The sunlight through lace makes beautiful shade
and your room looks more elegant.

Curtain Edging 4cm wide   Instructions on page 72
Lace Valance 102cm by 15.5cm   Instructions on page 73

Panel of Girl 30.5cm by 21cm   Instructions on page 74
Window Decoration 44.5cm by 38.5cm   Instructions on page 81

WHITE ACCENTS

Lamp Shade Cover and Matching Doily
Lamp Shade Cover 18.5cm high   Doily 23cm in diameter   Instructions on page 78

Pillows 40cm souare   Instructions on page 76

Bedspread 245cm by 165cm   Instructions on page 86

34   *Lace Pictures 13cm in inner diameter   Instructions on page 84*

BRIGHTEN YOUR TABLE

Tray Mat 36.5cm by 31cm   Instructions on page 90

Always keep laces neat and clean.
White lace brightens up the table.

Butterfly Tablecloth 110cm in diameter   Instructions on page 91

Flower Coasters 12.5cm in diameter   Instructions on page 94

Placemats 36cm by 26cm Instructions on page 94

Mats 20cm in diameter (Large mat), 16cm in diameter (Small mat)
Instructions on page 97

Ruffled Doily, *shown on page 1.*

MATERIALS: Mercerized crochet cotton, No. 40, 45 g white. Steel crochet hook size 0.90 mm.
FINISHED SIZE: 36 cm in diameter.
GAUGE: 1 dc = 0.5 cm.
DIRECTIONS: Begin at center. Make lp at the end of thread. Rnd 1: Ch 3, dc 17 in lp, end with sl st. Rnd 2: (Ch 3, dc 4) in same st, (ch 2, sk 2 dc, dc 5) 5 times, ch 2, end with sl st. Rnd 3: Ch 12, sk 3 dc, dc 1, (ch 2, sk 2 ch, dc 1, ch 9, sk 3 dc, dc 1) 5 times, ch 2, end with sl st. Rnd 4: Ch 3, dc 12, (ch 2, sk 2 ch, dc 13) 5 times, ch 2, end with sl st. Rnds 5–16: Work following chart. Dc 11 in 9-ch lp on every other rnd. Work in mesh pattern of 1 dc and 2 ch between 9 ch. Rnd 17: Work in sc all around. Cut off thread.

Make Flower Motifs. Ch 8. Join with sl st to form ring. Rnd 1: Ch 1, sc 16 in ring, end with sl st. Rnd 2: Ch 1, sc 1, (ch 3, sk 1 sc, sc 1) 8 times, end with sl st. Rnd 3: Ch 1, (sc 1, ch 3, dc 3, ch 3, sc 1) 8 times, end with sl st. Rnd 4: Sl st in back of work between petals. Repeat Rnds 3-4 through Rnd 7, joining Flower Motif to Center Circle. Make and join 18 Flower Motifs.
Attach thread at center petal of Flower Motif. Ch 1, sc 1, ch 9, dc 1, (dc 1, ch 9, sc 1, ch 9, dc 1) 17 times, dc 1, ch 9, end with sl st. Rnd 2: Ch 1, sc all around. Rnds 3-9: Work in mesh pattern. Rnd 10: Work in mesh pattern with 5-ch picot. Apply starch and press.

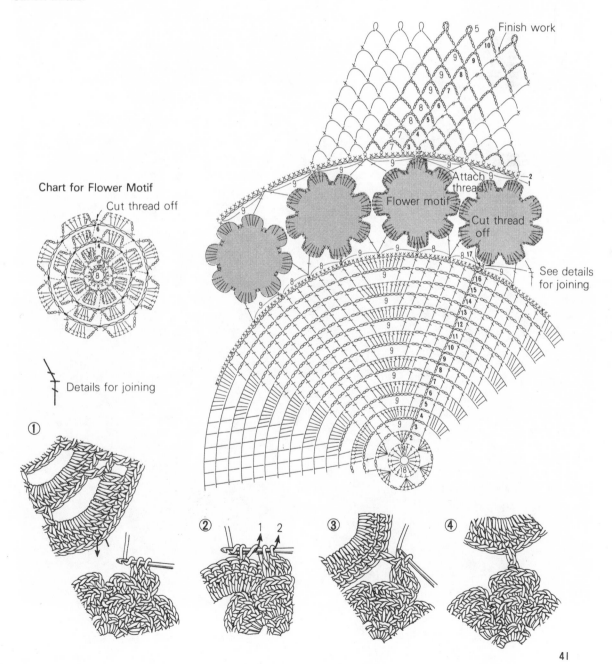

Chart for Flower Motif

Cut thread off

Details for joining

① ② ③ ④

Finish work

Attach thread

Flower motif

Cut thread off

See details for joining

41

Table Runner, *shown on page 2.*

MATERIALS: Mercerized crochet cotton, No. 40, 90 g white. Small amount of mercerized crochet cotton, No. 10, white for foundation thread. Steel crochet hook size 0.90 mm.
FINISHED SIZE: 115 cm by 33 cm.
GAUGE: 1 dc = 0.6 cm.

DIRECTIONS: Make Square Motifs in mesh pattern for background. Ch 41. Row 1: Ch 3, (ch 4, dc 1) 10 times. Rows 2–13: Work in mesh pattern following chart. Rnd 1: Ch 3, dc 42, ch 5, (dc 43, ch 5) 3 times, end with sl st. Rnds 2–4: Work in mesh pattern following chart. Cut off thread. Make 7 Square Motifs in same manner, joining motifs on Rnd 4 with sl st. Attach thread as indicated and work in mesh pattern with picots around Square Motifs. At the beginning of each rnd, sl st in back of picot. Increase on Rnds 5–6 as indicated. On Rnd 12, work in sc with picots and cut off thread.

ʌ=Attach thread
A=Cut thread off

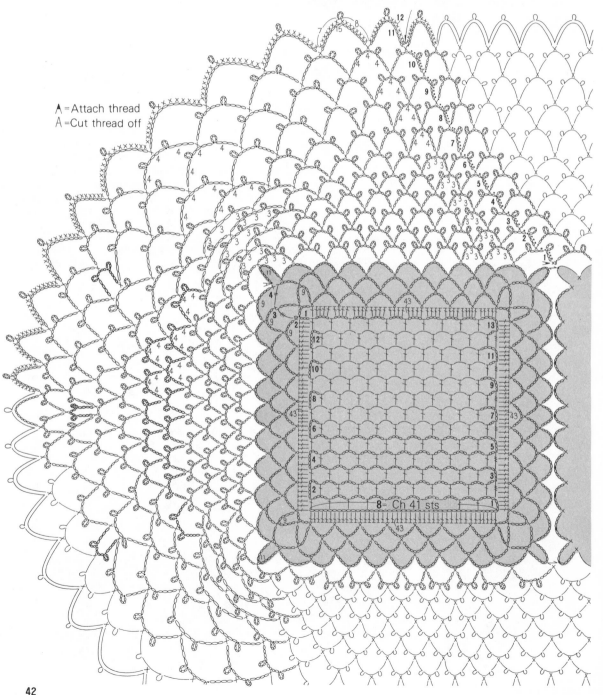

8= Ch 41 sts

For Motif A: Rnd 1: Sc 14 over foundation thread. Rnd 2: Ch 1, sc 14. Rnd 3: (Ch 2, dc 1) 4 times, ch 2, end with sl st. Rnd 4: Ch 1, sc 14 over foundation thread. Make 7 more petals in same manner, joining with 2 ch between petals. Sc 7 in each sc over foundation thread, sc 3 over foundation thread, sc 7 in each sc in same manner. Continue to work in sc all around.

For Motif A': Make triple loops with foundation thread. Sc 20 in triple lps. Rnds 2–3: Sc over 1 strand of foundation thread. Place Motif A' on center of Motif A and tack.

For Motif B: Make triple loops with foundation thread. Rnd 1: Ch 1, sc 18 in lps. Rnd 2: Sc 3 over 1 strand of foundation thread, make lp, with thread as shown in chart, sc 15 over thread. Make 6 lps and sc over lps in same manner. Cut off thread. Attach thread as indicated and work edging Repeat (sc 3, 4-ch picot, sc 2, 4-ch picot, sc 2, 4-ch picot, sc 2) over foundation thread in sc of lp, end with 2 sc over thread. Cut off thread. Make Stem. Sc 25 over foundation thread, ch 1, sc 25 over foundation thread in each sc. Attach stem in place. Make Leaf. Ch 11, (ch 1, sc 1, hdc 1, dc 7, hdc 1, sc 1, sl st) twice. Make two sets of Motif B, Stem, and Leaf.

For Motif C: Row 1: Sc 12 over foundation thread. Turn. Row 2: Ch 1, sc 10 in sc. Turn. Row 3: Ch 1, sc 10 in sc. Turn. Row 4: Ch 1, sc 10 over foundation thread, sc 2 in sc of Row 1, ch 1. Repeat Rows 1–4 to make 6 petals. Cut off thread. Attach thread for edging. Repeat (sc 3, 4-ch picot) in sc of petal 3 times, sc 1, (sc 2, 4-ch picot, sc 2) over both foundation threads, sc 1, (4-ch picot, sc 3) 3 times. Work in this manner all around. Make 2 Motif Cs.

For Motif C': Make triple loops with foundation thread. Sc 20 over lps. Ch 1, sc 1, repeat (sc 1, 4-ch picot, sc 1) over 1 strand of foundation thread, end with sl st. Place Motif C' on Motif C. Make 2 Motif C's.

For Motif D: Ch 8, sl st in first ch to form ring. Rnd 1: Ch 3, (ch 3 dc 1) 7 times, ch 3, end with sl st. Rnd 2: Ch 1, (sc 1, hdc 1, dc 3, hdc 1, sc 1) 8 times, end with sl st. Rnd 3: Ch 1, repeat (sc 1 in back of work between petals, ch 5), end with sl st. Rnds 4–8: Work as for Rnds 2–3. Make 2 Motif Ds. Make Leaf. Ch 15. Row 1: Ch 1, sc in both sides of ch. Rows 2–5: Work in ribbed st following chart. Make 4 Leaves. Attach leaves to flowers. After making all motifs, sew them in place as shown.

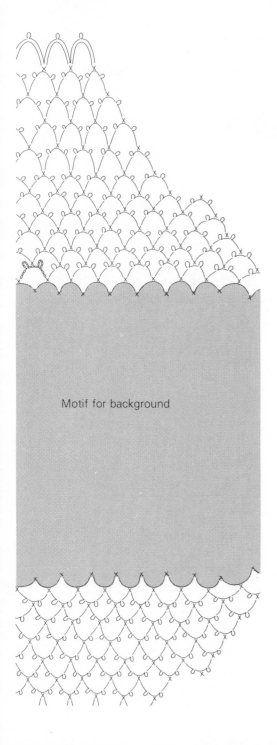

Motif for background

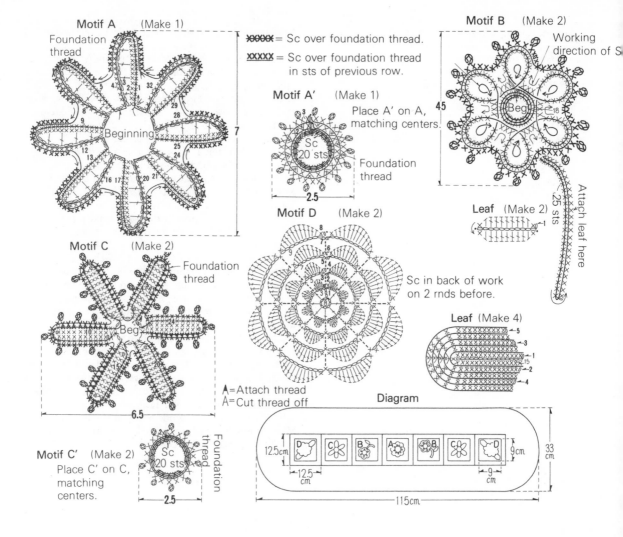

Motif A (Make 1)

Foundation thread

Beginning

XXXXX = Sc over foundation thread.

XXXXX = Sc over foundation thread in sts of previous row.

Motif A' (Make 1)

Place A' on A, matching centers.

Sc 20 sts

Foundation thread

2.5

Motif B (Make 2)

Working direction of S

Beg

Attach leaf here

25 sts

Leaf (Make 2)

Motif D (Make 2)

Sc in back of work on 2 rnds before.

Leaf (Make 4)

Motif C (Make 2)

Foundation thread

Beg

6.5

A = Attach thread
A = Cut thread off

Diagram

12.5cm | D | C | B | A | B | C | D | 9cm | 33 cm

12.5 cm | 9 cm

115cm

Motif C' (Make 2)

Place C' on C, matching centers.

Sc 20 sts

Foundation thread

2.5

Table Center, *shown on page 5.*

MATERIALS: Mercerized crochet cotton, No. 40, 45 g white. Steel crochet hook size 0.90 mm.
FINISHED SIZE: 52 cm by 32 cm.
GAUGE: 1dc = 0.6 cm.
SIZE OF MOTIFS: A: 10 cm in diameter; B: 5 cm in diameter.
DIRECTIONS: Make lp at the end of thread. Rnd 1: Ch 1, sc 8 in lp, end with sl st. Rnd 2: Ch 1, (sc 1, ch 30) 8 times, end with sl st. Cut off thread. Rnd 3: Attach thread at the top of 30-ch lp. Ch 3, dc 10, (dc 11, ch 4, dc 11) 7 times, dc 11, ch 2, dc 1. Rnds 4–5: Work in ch and dc following chart. Make second motif in same manner and join to first motif on Rnd 5.
For Motif B: Make lp at the end of thread. Rnd 1: Ch 1, dc 8 in lp, end with sl st. Rnd 2: Ch 1, (sc 1, ch 17) 4 times, end with sl st. Cut off thread. Attach thread at the top of 17-ch lp. Ch 3, dc 8, (dc 9, ch 2, sl st to join to Motif A, ch 2, dc 9) 3 times, dc 9, ch 2, sl st, ch 2, end with sl st. Cut off thread. Make 7 more Motif Bs, joining to Motif As. Attach thread at the corner of Motif A, and work 1 rnd of edging all around.

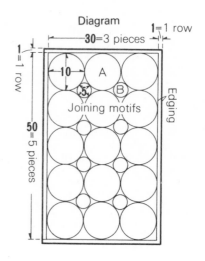

Diagram

1 = 1 row

30 = 3 pieces

1 = 1 row

10

A

5

B

50 = 5 pieces

Joining motifs

Edging

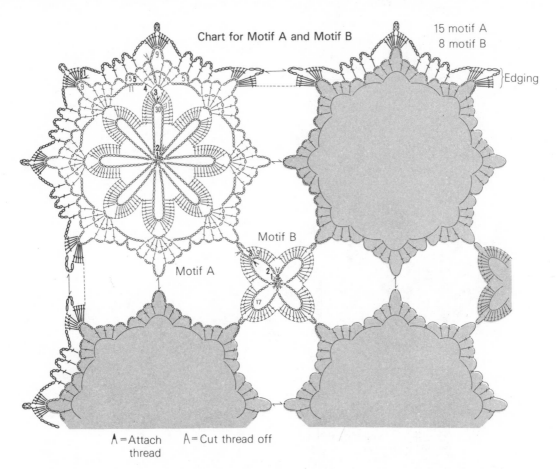

Chart for Motif A and Motif B

15 motif A
8 motif B

Edging

Motif B

Motif A

∧ = Attach thread   ⅄ = Cut thread off

Leaf-shaped Table Center, *shown on page 3.*

MATERIALS: Mercerized crochet cotton, No. 40, 100 g white. Steel crochet hook size 0.90 mm.
FINISHED SIZE: 77 cm by 44 cm.
GAUGE: 1 dc = 0.6 cm.
SIZE OF MOTIFS: Flower Motif A: 3.3 cm in diameter, B: 2.5 cm in diameter; Leaf Motif A: 4.3 cm by 2.8 cm, B: 4 cm by 2.5 cm.
DIRECTIONS: Begin at Center Flower. Ch 13. Join with sl st to form ring. Rnd 1: Ch 1, sc 14 in ring. Rnd 2: Ch 1, (sc 1, sc2 in 1 sc) 6 times, sc 2, end with sl st. There are 20 sts in all. Rnd 3: Ch 4, (ch 2, tr 1) 19 times, ch 2, end with sl st. Rnd 4: Ch 1, (sc 1, ch 1, dc 1, ch 1, sc 1) 20 times, end with sl st. Rnd 5: Ch 1, (sc 1, ch 3, sc 1 in back of sc) 19 times, ch 3, end with sl st. Rnd 6: Work as for Rnd 4, adding 2 more dc to each petal. Rnd 7: Ch 1, (sc 1, ch 3 sc 1 in back of work between petals, ch 10, sc 7 in each ch from 7th to 1st, sl st 1, ch 3) 9 times, end with sl st. Rnd 8: (ch 2, dc 1) 11 times, ch 2, sl st 1 for one petal. Make 10 petals. Rnd 9: Sc all around and cut off thread. Rnd 10: Place double strands of foundation thread around petals and work sc all around over foundation thread.
For Edging 1: Make 548 foundation ch and sl st to form ring. Rnd 1: Ch 3, (sc 1, ch 2, dc 1, ch 2, dc 1, ch 2) 91 times, sc 1, ch 2, dc 1, ch 1, hdc 1. Rnd 2: Ch 5, dc 1, (ch 2, dc 1, ch 2, dc 1) 92 times, ch 1, hdc 1. Rnds 3 – 8: Work in same manner as for Rnds 1 – 2, increasing number of ch.

For Stem: Ch 50. Sc on both sides of ch and join to Center Flower with sl st. Make one more stem for the other side.
For Flower Motif A: Ch 6, sl st in first ch to form ring. Rnd 1: Ch 3, (ch 3, dc 1) 5 times, ch 3, end with sl st. Rnd 2: Ch 1, (sc 1, hdc 1, dc 3, hdc 1, sc 1) 6 times, end with sl st. Rnd 3: Ch 1, (sc 1, ch 5, sc 1 in back of work between petals) 6 times, end with sl st. Rnd 4: Ch 1, (sc 1, hdc 1, dc 5, hdc 1, sc 1) 6 times, end with sl st. Rnd 5: Ch 1, (sc 1, ch 7, sc 1 in back of work between petals) 6 times, end with sl st. Rnd 6: Work in same manner as for Rnd 4, increasing dc joining to motifs and stems as indicated.
For Flower Motif B: Work as for Motif A through Rnd 4. Make Leaves and join Flower Motif Bs to Leaves.
For Leaves A & B: Ch 15. Row 1: Sc on both sides of ch Row 2: Work in ribbed st around sc of Row 1, adding 2 more sts at corner. Work through Row 8 for Leaf A, and Row 7 for Leaf B. On last Row, join Leaf A to Flower Motif A and Leaf B, and Leaf B to Edging 1 and Leaf A. Attach thread as indicated and join Leaves to Edging 1. Reverse Pattern for the left side and join Motifs to Center Flower in same manner.
For Edging 2: Ch 848. Work through Rnd 8 in same manner as for Edging 1, followed by mesh pattern with picots. Finish each rnd with dtr. Rnd 5: Repeat (sc 1, ch 10) all around. Rnd 6: Work in sc all around. Make and join 38 Flower Motif As between Edging 1 and Edging 2 as shown in chart.

45

x̲x̲x̲ Sc over foundation thread (2 strands of mercerized crochet cotton) in sts of previous row.

✕✕✕ Sc over foundation thread.

Edging 2

Edging 1

A

A

Flower motif
A

A

B

10

9

8

12

12

8 rows

7 rows

Leaf motif
A

B

Stem

Ch 50 sts

8 rows

7 rows

A

A

B

B

13

3

Center

46

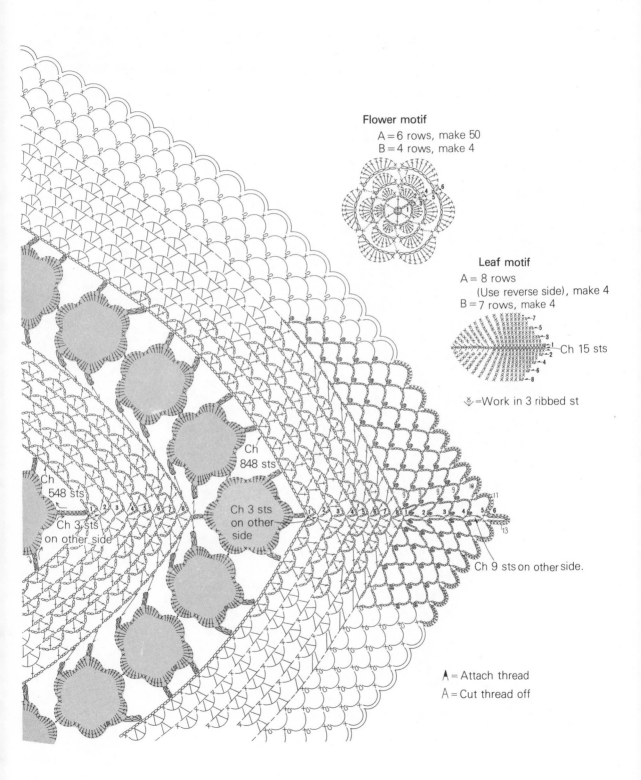

Flower motif

A = 6 rows, make 50
B = 4 rows, make 4

Leaf motif

A = 8 rows
(Use reverse side), make 4
B = 7 rows, make 4

Ch 15 sts

⚡=Work in 3 ribbed st

Ch 848 sts

Ch 548 sts

Ch 3 sts on other side

Ch 3 sts on other side

Ch 9 sts on other side.

A = Attach thread
A = Cut thread off

Table Center, *shown on page 4.*

MATERIALS: Crochet cotton, No. 40, 50 g white. Steel crochet hook size 0.90 mm.
FINISHED SIZE: 39 cm in diameter.
GAUGE: 1dc = 0.6 cm.

DIRECTIONS: Make lp at the end of thread. Rnd 1: Ch 3, dc 23 in lp, end with sl st. Rnd 2: Ch 3, (ch 2, dc 1) 11 times, ch 1, sc 1. Rnd 3: Repeat (sc 1, ch 5, 5-dc popcorn in sc) all around, end with 2 sl sts. Rnd 4: Ch 3, dc 3, (ch 3, dc 4 in 5-ch lp) 11 times, ch 3, end with sl st. Rnds 5–10: Work following chart. Dc 11 in 9-ch on Rnd 7, and 3 popcorns in 7-ch on Rnd 10. Rnds 11–14: Continue to work following chart. At the end of each rnd, ch 2 and dc 1 for 5 ch. Rnds 15–20: Work in same manner as for Rnds 3–6. Rnds 21–33: Work in same manner as for Rnds 7–17. Rnd 34: Work following chart and making 5-ch picot on top of each 5 dc. Cut off thread.

Square Doily, *shown on page 6.*

MATERIALS: Mercerized crochet cotton, No. 40, 25 g white. Steel crochet hook size 0.90 mm.
FINISHED SIZE: 29 cm square.
GAUGE: 1dc = 0.5 cm.

DIRECTIONS: Make lp at the end of thread. Rnd 1: Ch 3, dc 23 in lp. Rnd 2: Ch 3, (ch 3, dc 1) 11 times, ch 1, hdc 1. Rnd 3: (Sc 1, ch 5, 5-dc popcorn) 12 times, end with sl st. Rnd 4: Sl st 3, ch 3, dc 3, dc 4) 11 times, ch 3, end with sl st. Rnds 5–8: Work in same manner as for Rnd 4, following chart and making corners square. Rnds 9–23: Work following chart. Rnds 24–27: Work in mesh pattern of 9 ch. Rnd 28: Repeat (ch 4, sc 1 in 9-ch lp, 5-ch picot, ch 4, sl st 1) all around. End off.

Work in popcorn to bottom of sc.

Filet Mesh Table Runner, *shown on page 7.*

MATERIALS: Mercerized crochet cotton, No. 40, 180 g white. Steel crochet hook size 0.90 mm.
FINISHED SIZE: 124 cm by 43 cm.
GAUGE: 10 cm = 20 bls or sps; 10 cm = 20 rows.

DIRECTIONS: Beginning at bottom edge, ch 259. Turn each row. Work following chart. Repeat (Rows 23–67) 3 times after finishing Row 67. Continue to work Rows 203–248, as indicated.

49

43 = Ch 259 sts (86 bls + 1 st)

124 = 248 rows

Rose Pillows, *shown on page 9.*

MATERIALS: Quick crochet cotton (soft twisted) [same thickness as pearl cotton # 5], 290 g white. Steel crochet hook size 1.40 mm. Brown satin, 55 cm by 107 cm. Inner pillow stuffed with 750 g kapok, 55 cm square. 5 pairs of snap fasteners (medium).

FINISHED SIZE: 56 cm square.

GAUGE: 10 cm = 13 bls or sps; 10 cm = 13 rows.

DIRECTIONS: Beginning at the bottom edge, ch 193. Work in filet mesh for 64 rows, following chart. For Back, work in same manner as for Front without making rose pattern. Work 1 rnd each of sc around Front and Back pieces. Place Front on Back with wrong sides together, and stitch all around leaving 30 bls for opening. Work 3 rnds of edging on Front. Turn edging of Front toward you, work in ribbed st and sc for Front opening as indicated, and slip-stitch. For Back opening, work 1 rnd each of sc, ribbed st, and sc. Sew on 5 pairs of snap fasteners. Make inner pillow and cover with crocheted lace.

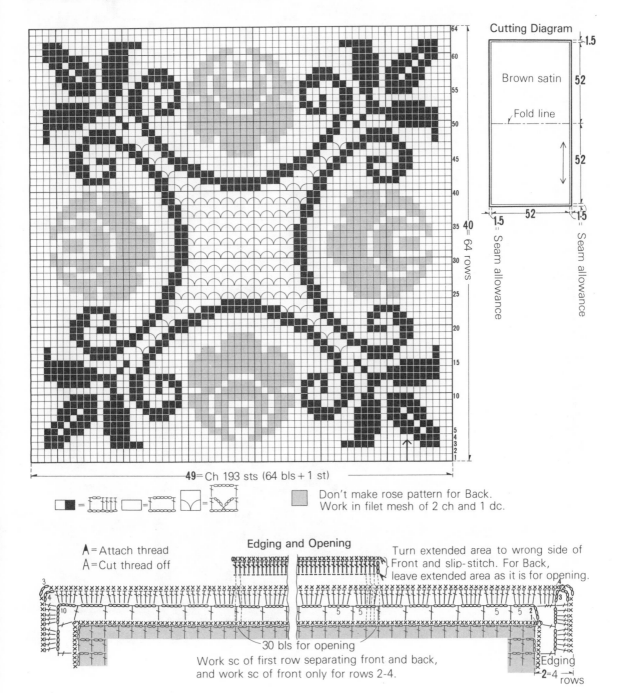

Cutting Diagram

Brown satin

Fold line

Seam allowance

= Ch 193 sts (64 bls + 1 st)

= Attach thread
= Cut thread off

Don't make rose pattern for Back.
Work in filet mesh of 2 ch and 1 dc.

Edging and Opening

Turn extended area to wrong side of Front and slip-stitch. For Back, leave extended area as it is for opening.

30 bls for opening

Edging

Work sc of first row separating front and back, and work sc of front only for rows 2-4.

Rose Tablecloth, *Shown on page 8*

MATERIALS: Quick crochet cotton (soft twisted) [Same thickness as pearl cotton # 5]. 730 g white. Steel crochet hook size 1.25 mm.

FINISHED SIZE: 133 cm square.

GAUGE: 10 cm = 12 bls or sps; 10 cm = 12 rows.

DIRECTIONS: Beginning at the bottom edge, ch 463. Work in filet mesh, following chart. After working for 154 rows, work 4 rnds of edging.

Edging

Heart-shaped Pillows, *shown on pages 10 & 11.*

MATERIALS: (for one pillow): Mercerized crochet cotton, No. 40, 50 g white. Steel crochet hook size 0.90 mm. Cross-stitch needle, No. 23. Pink (Purple) satin, 90 cm by 80 cm. Unbleached cotton fabric, 90 cm by 45 cm. Kapok, 200 – g. 3 pairs of snap fasteners (medium).
FINISHED SIZE: See diagram.
GAUGE: 1 dc = 0.6 cm.

DIRECTIONS: Make heart-shaped pattern following diagram. Make crocheted cords ①, ② and ③. Pin cords on pattern. Make and join motifs in numerical order. Work in herringbone stitch between cords ① and ②. Cut satin, adding 1 cm seam allowance. Make opening on Back. With right sides of Front and Back together, and ruffle in between, stitch all around. Turn to right side. Remove crocheted lace from pattern. Place lace on Front of satin pillow. Sew cords ① and ② to Front. Cut unbleached cotton fabric, 1 cm bigger than satin pillow and make inner pillow. Stuff with kapok.

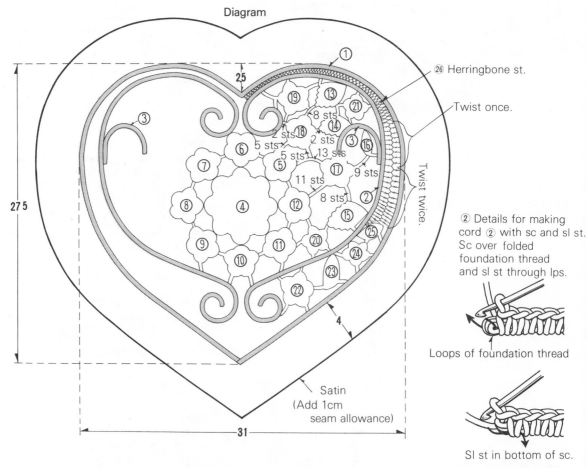

Diagram

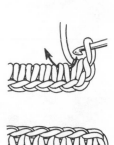

1. Make crocheted cord 92 cm long, following directions on page 96. Sl st all around, but sk 2 sts at center.
2. Fold 3 120 cm threads in half and sc over folded threads (see details at right).
3. Fold 3 16 cm threads in half and work in same manner as for 2. Pin cords 1, 2, and 3 on actual-size pattern with right side up.
4 – 12. Make and join motifs in numerical order.
13 – 16. Make and join motifs in numerical order.
17 – 18. Work in same manner as for 5, but decrease sts for joining.
19 – 25. Make and join motifs in numerical order.
26. Work in herringbone stitch between cords 1 and 2.

54

Join with sl st to cord ②.

Work sc on Rnds 3, 5, and 7 in back of work between petals of 2 previous rnds.

Sc over ch.

Work sc over foundation thread to previous rnds

Sc over foundation thread.

Ch 13 sts

∨ = ⋎

Join with sl st.

Ch 7 sts

Ch 10 sts

Ch 11 sts

See diagram for ⑰ – ⑱ .

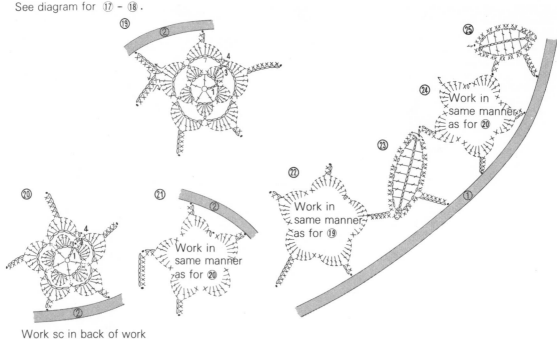

Work sc in back of work
between petals of Rnd 1.

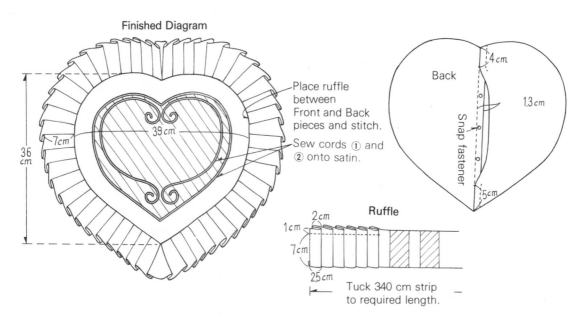

Finished Diagram

39 cm

7cm

36
cm

Place ruffle
between
Front and Back
pieces and stitch.

Sew cords ① and
② onto satin.

Back

4 cm

1.3 cm

Snap fastener

5cm

Ruffle

2 cm

1 cm

7 cm

25 cm

Tuck 340 cm strip
to required length.

Mesh Collar, shown on page 13.

MATERIALS: Mercerized crochet cotton, No. 40, 25 g white. Steel crochet hook size 0.90 mm. Small amount of crochet cotton, No. 10, white.
FINISHED SIZE: 38 cm on neck side and 10 cm wide.

GAUGE: 1 dc = 0.5 cm.
DIRECTIONS: Ch 201. Row 1: Repeat (dc 1, ch 1) to make 100 sps or bls. Rows 2–20: Work in mesh pattern with picots following chart. For Edging: Repeat (sc 11 in 9-ch lp, ch 11, sl st in 1st sc, sc 3, 3-ch picot, sc 2, 3-ch picot, sc 2, 3-ch picot, sc 2, 3-ch picot, sc 2, sl st in lp) all around. Work 1 row of sc on neck side.

For Flower Motif: Make lp at the end of thread. Rnd 1: Ch 3, (ch 3, dc 1) 5 times, ch 3, end with sl st. Rnd 2: Ch 1, (sc 1, hdc 1, dc 3 hdc 1, sc 1) in 3-ch lp 6 times, end with sl st. Rnd 3: Repeat (ch 5, sl st in back of work between petals) all around. Rnd 4: Repeat (sc 1, hdc 1, dc 5, hdc 1, sc 1) in 5-ch lp. Rnds 5–6: Work in same manner. Continue to work for stem. Ch 25. Sc over foundation thread, end with sl st. Make one more Flower Motif.

For Leaf: Ch 11. Sc on both sides of ch. Rows 2–4: Work in ribbed st following chart. Make 4 leaves. Attach Flowers and Leaves in place, curving stems as shown.

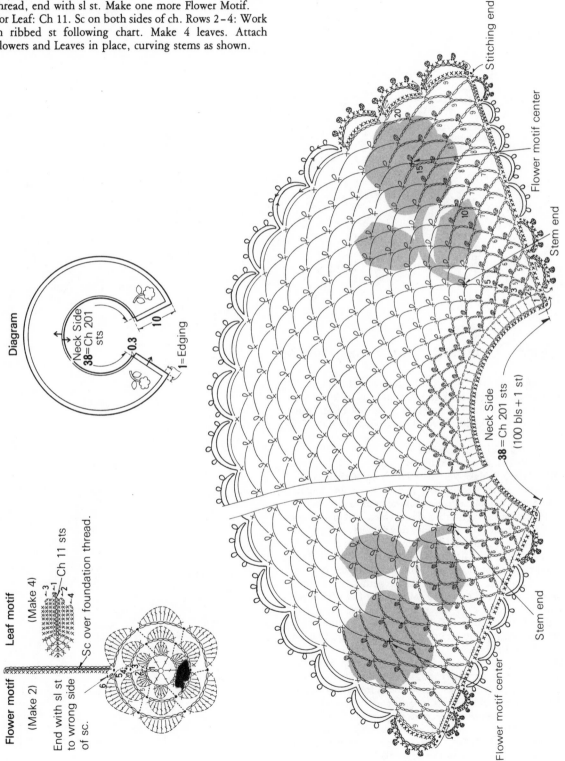

Diagram

Neck Side
38 = Ch 201 sts
0.3
10
1 = Edging

Neck Side
38 = Ch 201 sts
(100 bls + 1 st)

Stitching end
Flower motif center
Stem end
Stem end
Flower motif center

Flower motif

(Make 2)

End with sl st
to wrong side
of sc.

Leaf motif

(Make 4)

Ch 11 sts

Sc over foundation thread.

57

Scalloped Collar, *shown on page 12.*

MATERIALS: Mercerized crochet cotton, No. 40, 40 g white. Steel crochet hook size 0.90 mm.
FINISHED SIZE: 36.5 cm on neck side and 6.5 cm wide.
GAUGE: 1 dc = 0.5 cm.

DIRECTIONS: Ch 179. Row 1: Repeat (dc 1, ch 1) to make 89 sps or bls. Row 2: Repeat (dc 3, ch 2, 3-ch picot, ch 2, 3-ch picot, ch 1, dc 3, ch 2, dc 1, ch 2). Rows 3-11: Work following chart. Work 1 row of edging. End off.

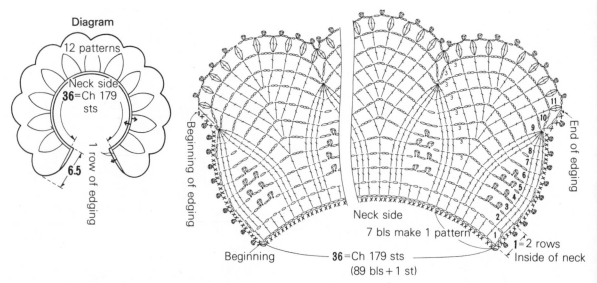

Doll Pochette, *shown on page 14.*

MATERIALS: Mercerized crochet cotton, No. 40, 10 g white. Steel crochet hook size 0.90 mm. Needle for embroidery. Navy blue velvet, 42 cm by 20 cm. Black satin, 42 cm by 19 cm. Golden cord, 0.2 cm in diameter and 7.9 m long.
FINISHED SIZE: See diagram.
GAUGE: Diameter of Motif A = 2 cm.
DIRECTIONS: Make 5 crocheted cords and 6 chain cords, following actual size pattern (see page 96 for making crocheted cord). Make required number of motifs from A to H, following each chart. Place cords and motifs on velvet and baste. Slip-stitch with tiny stitches, using white cotton sewing thread. Work in herringbone st with crochet cotton No. 40 for sleeves and sides of skirt. Embroider eyes, mouth and neck with crochet cotton No. 40. With right sides of Front and Back together, stitch three sides leaving top for opening. Make inner bag with black satin in same manner. Insert inner bag into outer bag with wrong sides together. Turn in seam allowance of inner bag and slip-stitch to turning of outer bag, 1 cm in from folded edge.
Braid 3 180 cm golden cords for shoulder strap. Leave 10 cm free for fringe at each end. Make braid for bottom, using 3 50 cm golden cords. Leave 10 cm free at each end. Add 4 15 cm golden cords to each end to make fringe. Make button following directions on page 60. Sew button in place. Make twisted cord for button loop, using 2 20 cm golden cords. Leave 4 cm free at ends. Attach button loop with golden sewing thread on Back.

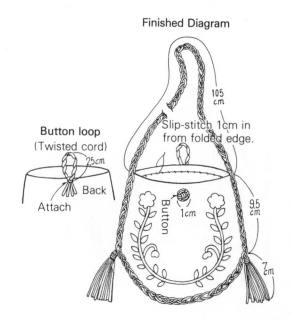

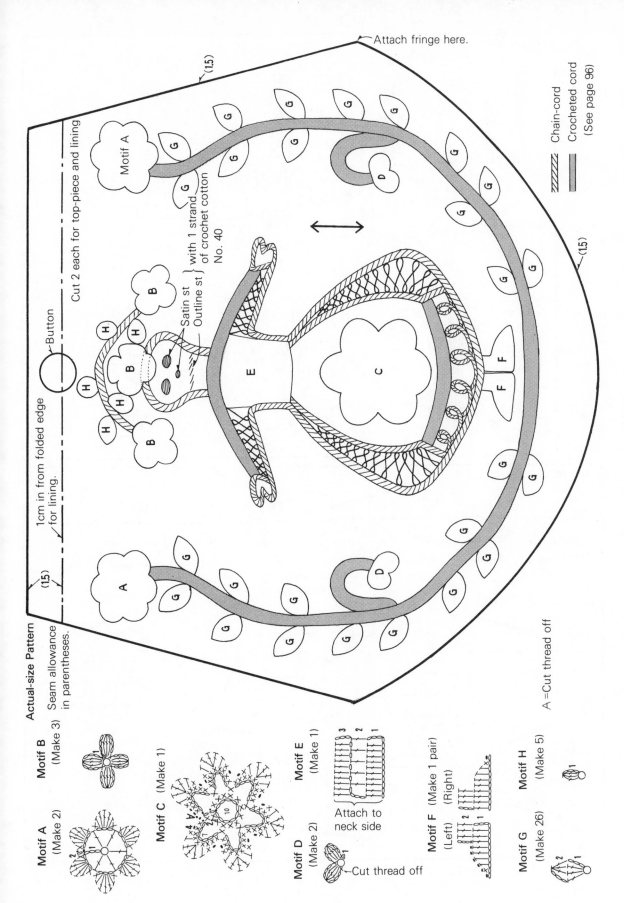

Attach fringe here.

(1.5)

Motif A

Button

1cm in from folded edge
for lining.

Cut 2 each for top-piece and lining

Satin st } with 1 strand
Outline st } of crochet cotton
No. 40

B

H H H
H B H
H H H
B

B

A

G G G G G G G G G G G G G G G G G G G G G G G G G G

D

D

E

C

F F
F F

Actual-size Pattern
Seam allowance
in parentheses.

(15)

(1.5)

(1.5)

A = Cut thread off

Chain-cord

Crocheted cord
(See page 96)

Motif A
(Make 2)

2 1

Motif B
(Make 3)

Motif C (Make 1)

4 3 2 1
10

Motif D
(Make 2)

Cut thread off

Motif E
(Make 1)

3
2
1

Attach to
neck side

Motif F (Make 1 pair)
(Right)

2 1

(Left)

Motif G
(Make 26)

2 1

Motif H
(Make 5)

1

59

How to Make Fringe:

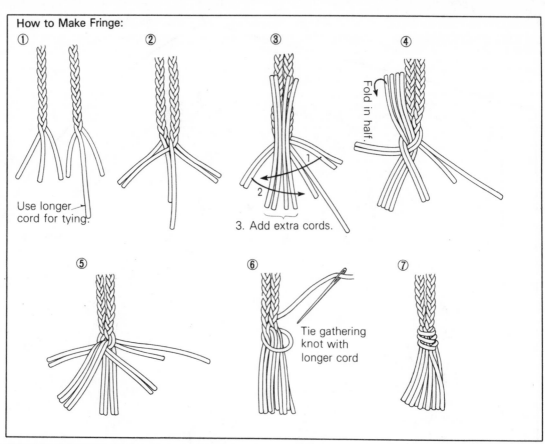

① Use longer cord for tying.

②

③ 3. Add extra cords.

④ Fold in half.

⑤

⑥ Tie gathering knot with longer cord

⑦

How to Make Button:

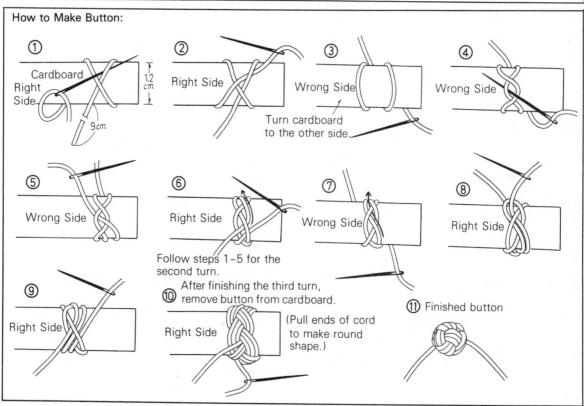

① Cardboard Right Side 1.2 cm 9cm

② Right Side

③ Wrong Side Turn cardboard to the other side.

④ Wrong Side

⑤ Wrong Side

⑥ Right Side Follow steps 1–5 for the second turn.

⑦ Wrong Side

⑧ Right Side

⑨ Right Side

⑩ After finishing the third turn, remove button from cardboard. Right Side (Pull ends of cord to make round shape.)

⑪ Finished button

Lace-trimmed Pochette, *shown on page 15.*

MATERIALS: Mercerized crochet cotton, No. 40, 5 g white. Steel crochet hook size 0.90 mm. Dark red velvet, 65 cm square. Dark red fabric for lining (inner bag), 45 cm by 16 cm. Pink round beads (small), 2 skeins. One pair of snap fasteners.

FINISHED SIZE: See diagram.

DIRECTIONS: Crochet 2 pieces of ruffle for bag and flap, working in mesh pattern with beads. The bead rows are worked from the wrong side, so use wrong side as front. Cut out velvet as indicated. With right sides of velvet together and crocheted ruffle in between, stitch three sides. Turn to right side.

Make inner bag. Insert inner bag into velvet bag with wrong sides together. Insert ends of shoulder strap between bags. Turn in seam allowance of inner bag and slip-stitch into velvet bag with wrong sides together. Insert ends of shoulder strap between bags. Turn in seam allowance of inner bag and slip-stitch along opening of velvet bag. Fold seam allowance of flap, place ruffle around flap, and lining on top. Slip-stitch. Sew flap in place with tiny stitches.

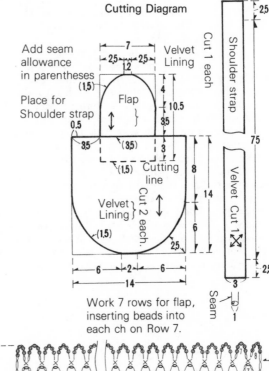

Cutting Diagram

Work 7 rows for flap, inserting beads into each ch on Row 7.

Ch 97 to make 32 sps or bls plus 1 st for 18 cm wide flap.
Ch 244 to make 81 sps or bls plus 1 st for 36 cm wide bag.
○ ...Thread beads at this mark for flap.
● ...Thread beads at this mark for bag.
(③...Thread 3 beads and sc.)
× ...Sc in marked ch.

Shoulder strap 75 cm long

Place seam line on inside.

Place lining 0.5 cm in from edge and slip-stitch.

Place lining 2 cm in from edge and slip-stitch.

A = Cut thread off

Cover snap fasteners with lining fabric.

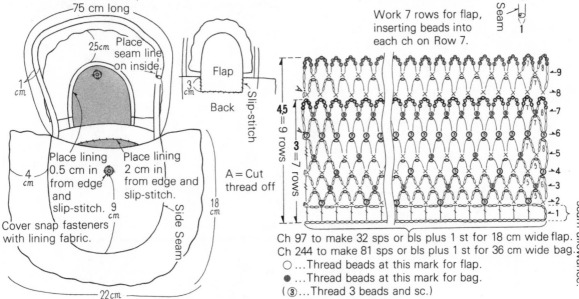

How to Crochet with Beads

How to sc with beads

2nd row
1st row

How to ch with beads

Last row

2nd row
1st row

61

Piano Cover, *shown on pages 16 & 17.*

MATERIALS: Mercerized crochet cotton, No. 40, 220 g white. Crochet cotton, No. 10, 26-g white. Steel crochet hook size 0.90 mm. White linen, 154 cm by 47 cm.
FINISHED SIZE: See diagram.
GAUGE: 10 cm = 15 bls or sps; 10 cm = 20 rows.
DIRECTIONS: Draw one thread each vertically and horizontally from white linen, 0.3 cm from edge. Fold edges from thread-drawn line, refold (0.3 cm hem) and press. Sc all around, working 3 sc at corners. Attach thread and work for filet mesh background. Make 228 bls or sps and work even through Row 29. Attach thread and work for scalloped edge — work 4 rows at sides, and 11 rows for 8 scallops. Attach thread and work 1 rnd of sc and another rnd of (sc 1, 3-ch picot, sc 1) all around.
For Small Flowers: Ch 4, sl st in first ch to form ring. Rnd 1: Ch 3, (ch 3, dc 1) 5 times, ch 3, end with sl st. Rnd 2: Ch 1, repeat (sc 1, hdc 1, dc 3, hdc 1, sc 1) in 3-ch lp 6 times, end with sl st. Rnd 3: Repeat (ch 5, sl st in back of work between petals) 6 times. Rnds 4-6: Work as for Rnds 2-3, but join to picot of edging with sl st on Rnd 6. Make and join second flower in same manner. Make and join 57 flowers.

For Motif A: Make outer petals first. Ch 15. Work in sc on Row 1, in ribbed st on Rows 2-3. Sl st 7 each at the beginning and ending of Row 3. Make second petal in same manner, starting with 17 ch. Sl st 7 in each sl st of first petal to join. Make 3 more petals in same manner. Cut off thread. Make inner petals. Make double loops with foundation thread. Sc 12 over lps. Work as for Small Flower, but join to outer petals with sl st on Rnd 4. Place foundation thread around Motif A and work edging over thread. Make 8 Motif As.
For Motif B: Make lp at the end of thread and work following chart. Make 8 Motif Bs with 6 petals.
For Motif C: Make double loops with foundation thread. Sc 20 over lps. Cut off foundation thread. Work through Rnd 4, following chart and working over foundation thread on Rnd 4. Make 8 Motif Cs.
For Motif D: Ch 13. Work in sc on Row 1, in ribbed st on Rows 3-5, following chart. Make 32 Motif Ds.
For Motifs E & F: Work as for Motif D. Make 8 Motifs each.
For Stem: Work over foundation thread in sc following chart. Form stem by pulling foundation thread. Place finished motifs on filet mesh back ground and tack them without showing stitches.

Diagram

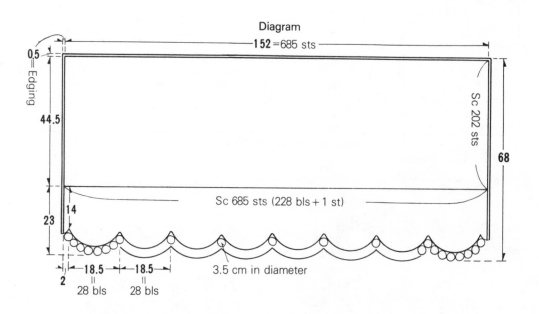

152 = 685 sts

0.5 = Edging

44.5

Sc 202 sts

68

Sc 685 sts (228 bls + 1 st)

14

23

18.5   18.5

2

28 bls   28 bls

3.5 cm in diameter

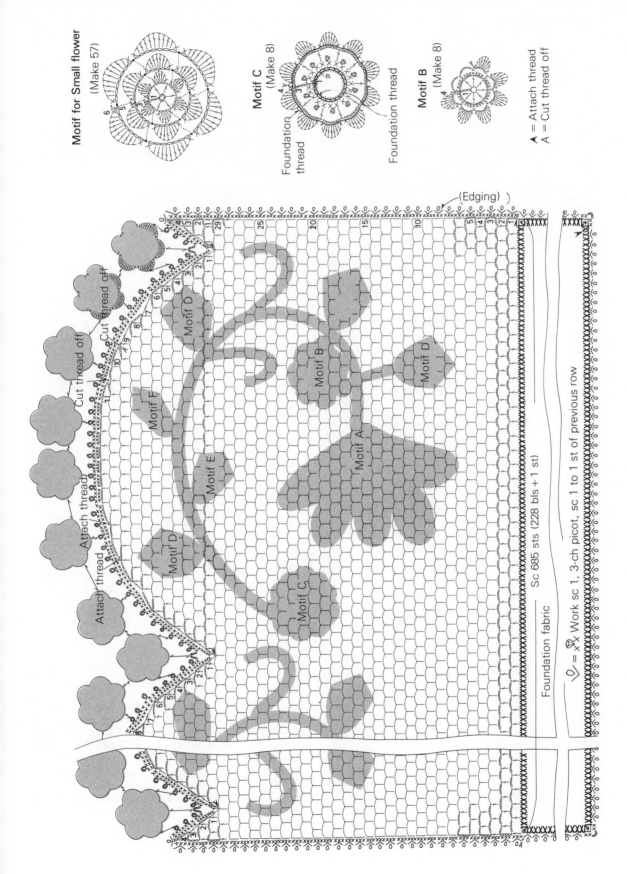

Motif for Small flower
(Make 57)

Motif C
(Make 8)

Foundation thread

Foundation thread

Motif B
(Make 8)

A = Attach thread
A = Cut thread off

(Edging)

Cut thread off

Cut thread off

Attach thread

Attach thread

Attach thread

Motif D

Motif F

Motif E

Motif D

Motif C

Motif B

Motif A

Motif D

Sc 685 sts (228 bls + 1 st)

Foundation fabric

▽ = ⤬⤬ Work sc 1, 3-ch picot, sc 1 to 1 st of previous row

63

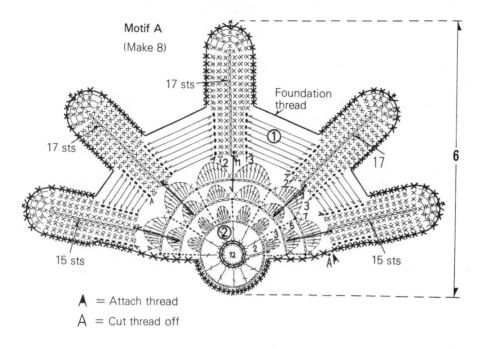

Motif A
(Make 8)

17 sts

Foundation thread

①

17 sts

17

15 sts

A

15 sts

A = Attach thread

A = Cut thread off

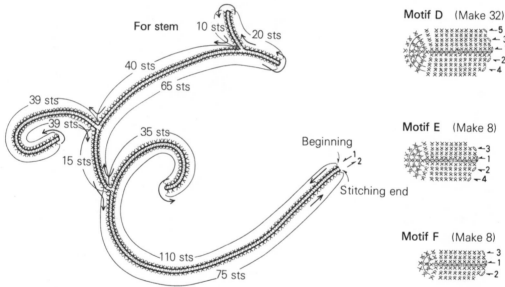

For stem

10 sts

20 sts

40 sts

65 sts

39 sts

39 sts

35 sts

15 sts

Beginning

1

2

Stitching end

110 sts

75 sts

Motif D (Make 32)

←5
←3
←1
←2
←4

Motif E (Make 8)

←3
←1
←2
←4

Motif F (Make 8)

←3
←1
←2

Daisy Doily, shown on page 18.

MATERIALS: Mercerized crochet cotton, No. 40, 30 g white. Steel crochet hook size 0.90 mm.
FINISHED SIZE: 32 cm in diameter.
GAUGE: 1 dc = 0.6 cm.
DIRECTIONS: Ch 8, sl st in first ch to form ring. Rnd 1: Ch 1, sc 12 in ring, end with sl st. Rnd 2: Repeat (sc 1, ch 5) 5 times, sc 1, ch 2, hdc 1. Rnd 3: Repeat (5-dc popcorn, ch 5) 12 times, hdc 1. Rnd 5: Repeat (sc 1, ch 25, sc 1, ch 5) 12 times, end with sl st. Rnd 6: Work in dc and ch following chart. Cut off thread. Rnd 7: Attach thread. Repeat [(sc 1, 5-ch picot, ch 11, sl st, 5-ch picot) in 3-ch lp, ch11] 12 times and cut off thread. Rnds 8–11: Attach thread. Work in sc ch and dc following chart. Rnds 12–13: Work as for Rnds 5–6. Cut off thread. Rnd 14: Attach thread. Repeat (dc 7, ch 7) in 3-ch lp around. Rnd 15; Repeat (7-dc cluster, ch 7, sc 1, 3-ch picot, ch 7) around. Rnds 16–20: Work in mesh pattern with 3-ch picot in each sc. End off.

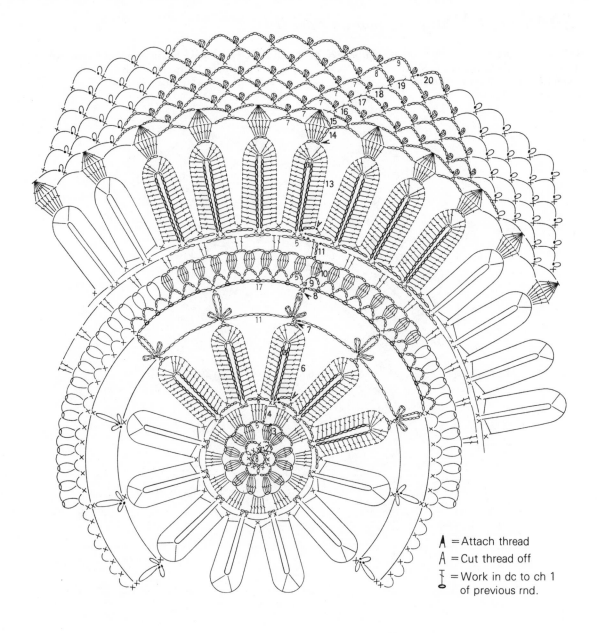

$\bigwedge$ = Attach thread

$\bigwedge$ = Cut thread off

$\underset{\bullet}{\overline{\underline{\text{I}}}}$ = Work in dc to ch 1 of previous rnd.

Sunflower Doily, *shown on page 19.*

MATERIALS: Mercerized crochet cotton, No. 40, 20 g
white. Steel crochet hook size 0.90 mm.
FINISHED SIZE: 30 cm in diameter.
GAUGE: 1 dc = 0.5 cm.

DIRECTIONS: Make lp at the end of thread. Rnd 1: Ch
3, dc 23 in lp, end with sl st. Rnds 2 – 24: Work in dc, ch,
sc and sl st, following chart. End off.

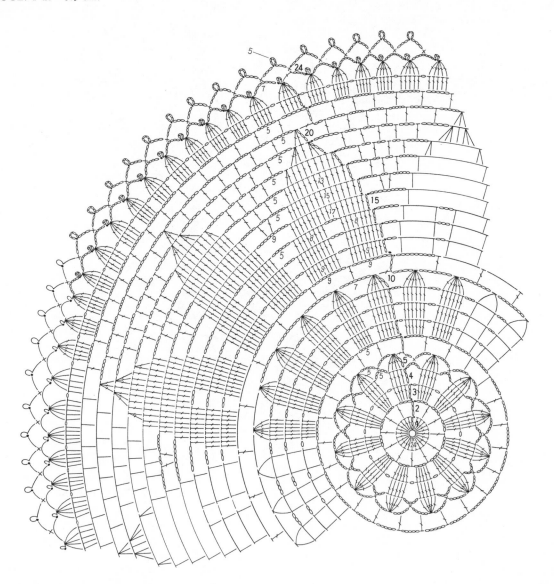

Doily, *Shown on page 22.*

MATERIALS: Mercerized crochet cotton, No. 40, 30 g
white. Steel crochet hook size 0.90 mm.
FINISHED SIZE: 30 cm in diameter.
GAUGE: 1 dc = 0.5 cm.

DIRECTIONS: Ch 6, join with sl st to form ring. Rnd 1:
Ch 3, (ch 3, dc 1) 7 times, ch 3, end with sl st. Rnds 2 – 4:
Work in ch and dc, increasing as shown in chart. Rnd 5:
Repeat (sc 1, ch 8, 5-dc popcorn in third ch, 5-dc popcorn, ch 5, 5-dc popcorn, ch 3) around. Rnd 6: Repeat (dc
2, ch 7, 5-dc popcorn, ch 7) to complete flowers. Rnds
7 – 21: Work in ch, dc, sc and sl st, following chart. Rnds
22 – 23: Work as for Rnds 5 – 6. Rnds 24 – 28: Work in
mesh pattern of 7-ch and sc. End off.

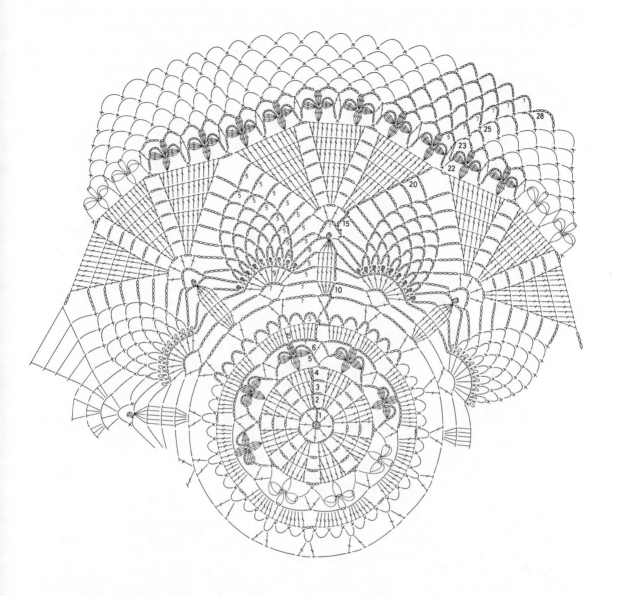

Breughel Lace Doily, *shown on page 20.*

MATERIALS: Mercerized crochet cotton, No. 40, 35 g white. Steel crochet hook size 0.90 mm.
FINISHED SIZE: 43 cm by 30 cm oval.
GAUGE: 1 dc = 0.6 cm.
DIRECTIONS: Work in numerical order from 1 to 8.
1. Make braid in dc and ch. Row 1: Ch 10, dc in 6th ch, dc 4 in each ch. Turn. Row 2: Ch 5, dc 5. Turn. Row 3: Repeat Row 2. Rows 4–32: Work as for Rows 2–3. Join ends after Row 32, following directions on page 98.

2. Make lp at the end of thread. Rnd 1: Repeat (3-dc cluster, ch 3) 8 times (counts 1st 3 ch as 1 dc and last 1 ch and 1 hdc as 3 ch). Rnd 2: Repeat (sc 1, ch 3, dc 2 in each lp of braid, ch 3) around. Cut off thread. Make second braid, joining to first braid as shown with sl st. Make and join 3 motifs in this manner.
3. Make braid as for step 1, but increase sts—7 dc and 7 ch for outside and 5 ch for inside.
4. Rnd 1: Attach thread at lp of braid of step 1. Repeat (sc 1, ch 3, 3-ch picot, ch 7, 3-ch picot, ch 3, sc 1, ch 2, 3-ch picot, ch 2) around. Repeat (ch 3, 3-ch picot ch 2) between motifs. Cut off thread, after finishing one rnd. Rnd 2: Attach thread again and work as for Rnd 1, joining to 7-dc braid of step 3 with sl st as shown in chart.

5. Make 5-dc braid as for step 1. On Row 5, join to lp of braid of step 3 with sc. On Row 8, ch 2, sc in 3 lps together. On Row 17, join to lp of braid as for Row 5. Work in this manner through Row 307. On Row 308, join to Row 1.

6. Attach thread at lp of braid of step 3. Work and join to braids of 3 and 5, following chart. Cut off thread. Fill inside of braid in this manner—10 places.

7. Work as for step 6. Work Row 1 of step 6 in lp of braid. Fill inside of braid at corners—4 places.

8. Attach thread at lp of braid of step 5. Repeat (dc 1, ch 3) twice in lp. Omit ch 3 between 2 dc at the concave. Work as for Rnd 1, increasing number of ch. Work one more rnd in same manner, adding picots. End off.

Rose Doily, *shown on page 21.*

MATERIALS: Mercerized crochet cotton, No. 40, 30 g white. Steel crochet hook size 0.90 mm.
FINISHED SIZE: 31 cm in diameter.
GAUGE: 1 dc = 0.5 cm.
DIRECTIONS: Beginning at center, make lp at the end of thread. Rnd 1: Ch 3, dc 23 in lp, end with sl st. Rnd 2: (Ch 3, dc 4) in sl st, (ch 2, dc 5) 5 times, ch 2, end with sl st. Rnd 3: Ch 12, dc 1, ch 2, (dc 1, ch 9, dc 1, ch 2) 5 times, end with sl st. Rnd 4: Ch 3, dc 10 in 9-ch lp, (dc in dc, dc 2 in 2-ch lp, dc in dc, dc 11 in 9-ch lp) 5 times, dc in dc, dc 2 in 2-ch lp, end with sl st. Rnds 5 – 11: Work following chart. Cut off thread.

For Rose: Make lp at the end of thread. Rnd 1: Ch 3, (ch 3, dc 1) 5 times, ch 3, end with sl st. Rnd 2: Ch 1, (sc 1, hdc 1, dc 3, hdc 1, sc 1) in each lp, end with sl st. Rnd 3: Ch 4, sl st in back of sc between petals. Rnds 4 – 5: Work as for Rnds 2 – 3, increasing sts. Rnd 6: Make petals with picots. Join 2 picots to Rnd 11 of Center Circle. Make and join 12 Roses.
For Border: Attach thread. Rnd 1: Repeat (sc 1, ch 11, sc 1, ch 17) around. Rnd 2: Repeat (sc in sc, sc 13 in 11-ch lp, sc in sc, sc 17 in 17-ch lp, sc in sc) around. Rnds 3 – 8: Work in mesh pattern. Rnd 9: Work in mesh pattern with 5-ch picots. Starch and ruffle.

How to make motif

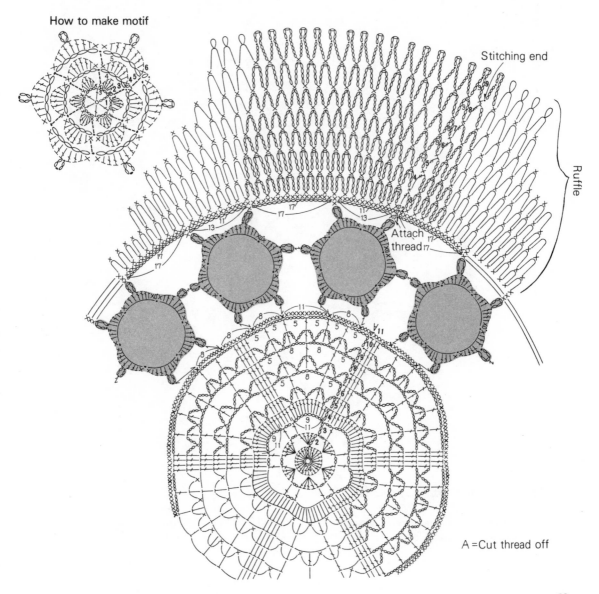

Stitching end

Ruffle

Attach thread

A =Cut thread off

Doily, *shown on page 23.*

MATERIALS: Mercerized crochet cotton, No. 40, 25 g white. Steel crochet hook size 0.90 mm.
FINISHED SIZE: 29 cm in diameter.
GAUGE: 1 dc = 0.6 cm.

DIRECTIONS: For Motif A: Ch 6, join with sl st to form ring. Rnd 1: Ch 1, sc 12 in ring. Rnds 2–8: Work following chart. Work sl st in back of work of 2 preceding rnds on Rnds 4, 6, and 8. Make 7 Motif As.
For Motif B: Attach thread at Rnd 8 of Motif A. Work following chart. Join to Center Motif A with sl st on Rnd 4. Make second Motif B and join to first Motif B and to Center Motif A on Rnd 4. Make and join 6 Motif Bs. Work 9 rnds edging all around.

Motif A

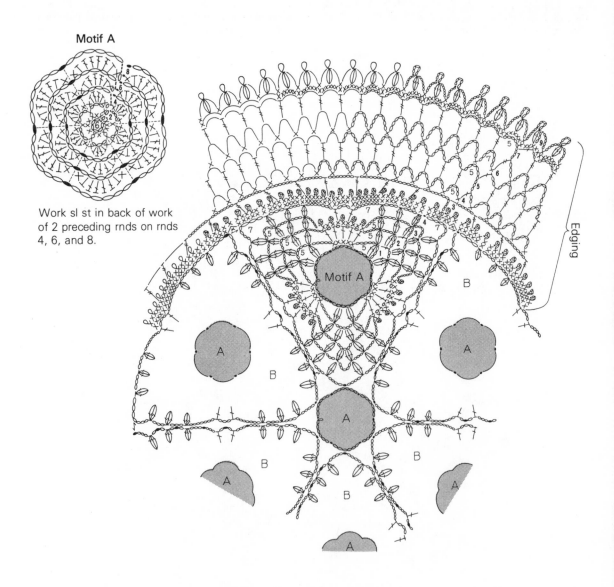

Work sl st in back of work of 2 preceding rnds on rnds 4, 6, and 8.

Doily, *shown on page 24.*

MATERIALS: Mercerized crochet cotton, No. 40, 40 g white. Steel crochet hook size 0.90 mm.

FINISHED SIZE: 35 cm in diameter.
GAUGE: 1 dc = 0.5 cm.

DIRECTIONS: Work in numberical order from 1 to 5.
1. Ch 5. Repeat (ch 5, dc 5 in 5-ch, ch 5, dc 1, ch 1, dc 1, ch 1, dc 1) through Row 20. Row 21: Ch 2, sl st in 3 lps, ch 3. Row 64: Join to lp of Row 6 with sl st. Row 66: Join to lp of Row 4 with sl st. Make loops with braid, overlapping left braid on right braid at bottom. After finishing Row 272, join to Row 1, following directions on page 98. Cut off thread.
2. Attach thread as indicated. Repeat (ch 3, sc 1, 3-ch and 2-dc cluster, sc 1) 4 times, ch 3, end with sl st. Cut off thread. Fill inside of braid loops in this manner.

3. Ch 8, join with sl st to form ring Rnd 1: Ch 1, sc 16 in ring. Rnd 2: Repeat (5-dc popcorn, ch 5) 8 times (counts 1st 3-ch as 1 dc and last 2-ch and 1-hdc as 5 ch). Rnd 3: Repeat (sc 1, ch 4, sl st in lp, ch 4, sc 1) 8 times, end with sl st. Cut off thread.
4. Make braid as for step 1. Work 128 rows, joining to top of braid lps. Join ends of braid to form ring.
5. Attach thread as indicated. Work following chart through Rnd 13.
For Motif A: Ch 8, join with sl st to form ring. Rnd 1: Ch 1, sc 16 in ring. Rnd 2: Repeat (5-dc popcorn, ch 5) around, joining to lps of braid as indicated. Rnd 3: Ch 2, sl st in lp. Turn. Rnd 4: Work in hdc and dc. Sl st in lp of outer braid. Make and join 8 Motif As.

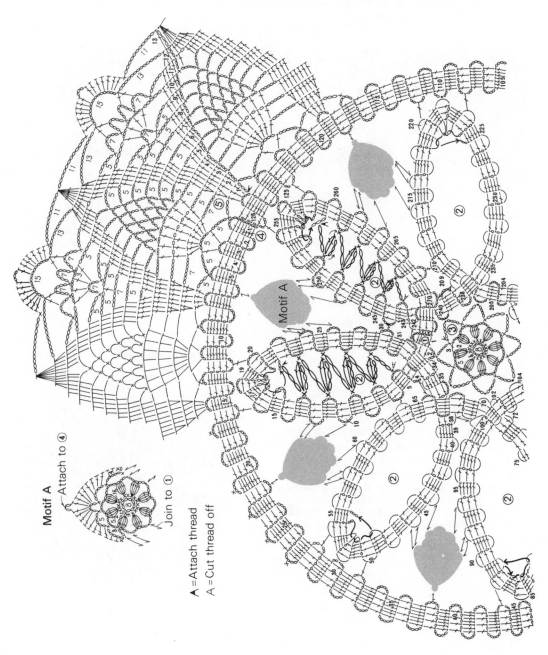

Curtain Edging, *shown on page 26.*

MATERIALS: (for one side): Mercerized crochet cotton, No. 40, 50 g white. Steel crochet hook size 0.90 mm.
FINISHED SIZE: See diagram.
GAUGE: 1 dc = 0.5 cm.

DIRECTIONS: Ch 821. Work for 10 rows following chart. Rows 5–7: Work in pattern st. Rows 8–10: Work in mesh pattern. Attach thread as indicated and work 1 row for edging. Make another piece in same manner. Adjust length depending on the length of curtain. You may need professional help for finished curtain.

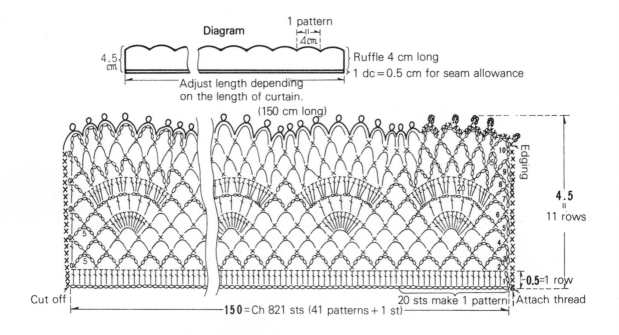

Doily, *shown on page 25.*

MATERIALS: Mercerized crochet cotton, No. 40, 30 g white. Steel crochet hook size 0.90 mm.
FINISHED SIZE: 31.5 cm in diameter.
GAUGE: 1 dc = 0.6 cm.
DIRECTIONS: Work in numerical order from 1 to 3.
1. Make braid. Ch 5. Repeat (ch 7, dc 5 in each ch, ch 5, dc 5) through Row 48. Join ends following directions on page 98. Cut off thread.
2. Ch 8, join with sl st to form ring. Rnd 1: Ch 3, dc 23 in ring, end with sl st. Rnd 2: Repeat (sc 1, ch 11, sl st in lp of braid, ch 2, dc 9 in each ch) in every other dc, 12 times. Cut off thread. Attach thread as indicated and work for another rnd to make petals again. Repeat Rnd 2, pressing petals of Rnd 2 toward you. Cut off thread.
3. Attach thread. Repeat (sc in lp of braid, ch 7) around. Rnds 2–18: Work following chart. Rnd 19: Work in ch with 5-ch picots. End off.

Chart for Second petals

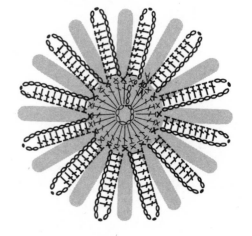

A = Attach thread
A = Cut thread off

Lace Valance, *shown on page 27.*

MATERIALS: Mercerized crochet cotton, No. 40, 50 g
white. Steel crochet hook size 0.90 mm.
FINISHED SIZE: 102 cm by 15.5 cm.
GAUGE: 1 dc = 0.5 cm.

DIRECTIONS: Ch 595. Row 1: Ch 3, dc 1 in each ch.
Row 2: Ch 3, repeat (dc 1; ch 2) to make 198 bls or sps.
Rows 3–32: Work following chart. Work 1 row of edging
on three sides. End off.

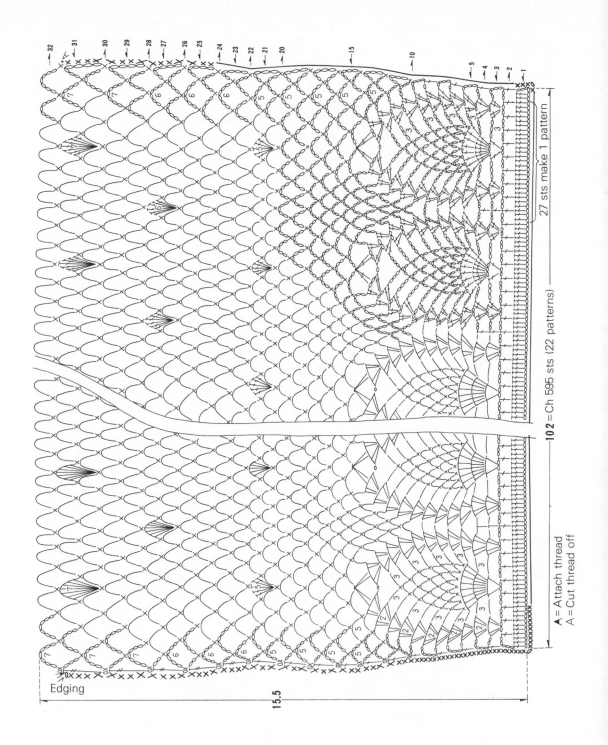

Panel of Girl, *shown on page 28.*

MATERIALS: Mercerized crochet cotton, No. 40, 25 g white. Steel crochet hook size 0.90 mm.
FINISHED SIZE: 30.5 cm by 21 cm oval.
GAUGE: 10 cm = 19.5 bls or sps; 10 cm = 20 rows.

DIRECTIONS: Begining at bottom edge, ch 22. Work in filet mesh following chart. Increase on right and left sides on Rows 1–15 and decrease on Rows 48–61.

21 = 41 blocks

61

60

55

50

47

45

40

35

30

25

20

15

10

5

3

1

30.5
=
61 rows

4 = Ch 22 sts
(7 bls + 1 st)

=

=

Work in ch

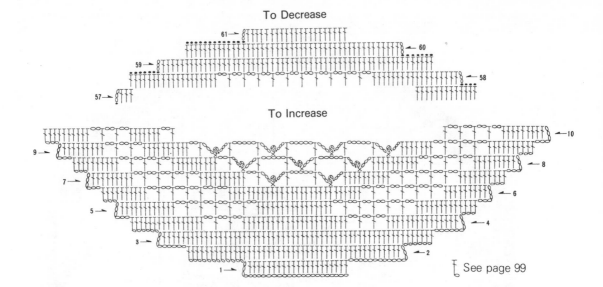

To Decrease

To Increase

See page 99

Pillows, *shown on page 31.*

MATERIALS: (for one pillow): Mercerized crochet cotton, No. 40, 100 g white. Steel crochet hook size 0.90 mm. Coffee brown (Blue) satin, 86 cm by 44 cm. Inner pillow stuffed with 450 g kapok, 40 cm square.
FINISHED SIZE: 40 cm square.
GAUGE: 10 cm = 18 bls or sps; 10 cm = 18 rows.

DIRECTIONS: Make Front. Ch 223. Row 1: Repeat (ch 2, dc 1) to make 74 bls or sps. Rows 2–74: Work in filet mesh following chart. For Back, ch 408. Join with sl st to form square. Work for 20 rnds, increasing at corners as shown. Work 1 rnd of edging inside foundation ch (see Edging ①). With wrong sides of Front and Back together, sc all around. Work 3 more rnds for edging (see Edging ②). Make 85 cm long cord in ch st using 3 strands. Add extra strands at each end of cord for fringe. Trim excess beyond 2 cm from knot. Run cord through sps of Rnd 1 of Back piece.

Increasing corners of Back and Edging ①

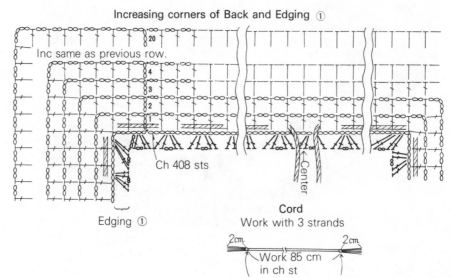

Inc same as previous row.

Ch 408 sts

Edging ①

Center

Cord
Work with 3 strands

Work 85 cm in ch st

Put 5 strands each of 6 cm-thread into first and last sts. Fold in half and tie knot. Trim excess beyond 2 cm from knot.

See chart for inc on page 76

Back

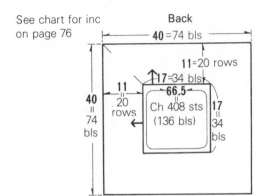

40 = 74 bls

11 = 20 rows

17 = 34 bls

66.5

Ch 408 sts
(136 bls)

11
||
20 rows

40
||
74
bls

17
||
34
bls

Edging ②

(With wrong sides of Front and Back together, sc all around on Row 1.)

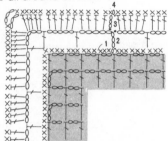

Front

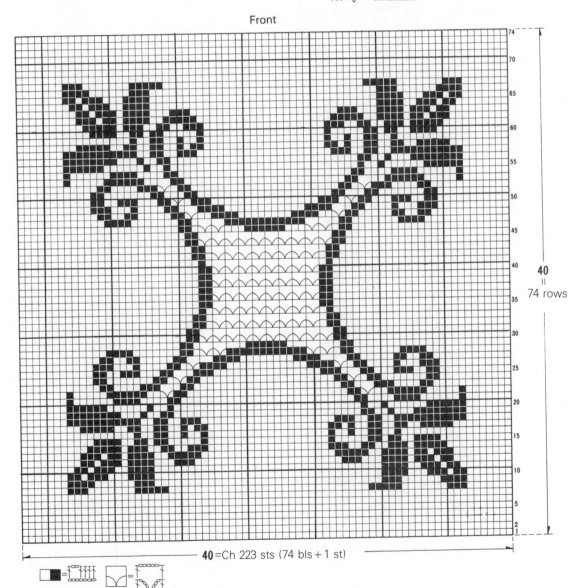

40
||
74 rows

40 = Ch 223 sts (74 bls + 1 st)

Lamp Shade Cover and Matching Doily, *shown on page 30.*

Lamp shade

MATERIALS: Mercerized crochet cotton, No. 40, 55 g beige. Steel crochet hook size 0.90 mm. Lamp shade: 14 cm in diameter at top, 23 cm in diameter at bottom, and 18.5 cm high.

FINISHED SIZE: See diagram.

DIRECTIONS: Ch 241. Join with sl st to form ring. Work for 54 rnds in mesh pattern of 5-ch, increasing on Rnds 12, 24, 37 and 51. Attach thread at top and bottom, and work 1 rnd each for edging.

For Motif A: Ch 8. Join with sl st to form ring. Rnd 1: Ch 1, sc 16 in ring, end with sl st. Rnd 2: Repeat (sc 1, ch 12, dc 7 in each ch) 8 times. Cut off thread. Make 8 Motif As.

For Motif B: Ch 12. Join with sl st to form ring. Rnd 1: Ch 1, sc 12 in ring, end with sl st. Rnd 2: Repeat (sc 1, ch 9, sc 1, ch 7) 6 times. Rnd 4: Turn motif, so that crochet hook is on your side. Repeat (sc 1, 3-ch picot, ch 2) 6 times. Cut off thread. Rnd 5: Attach thread. Repeat (sc 1 in 7-ch lp, ch 5, sc 1 in dc, ch 5) around. Cut off thread. Make 8 Motif Bs.

For Motif C: Ch 6. Join with sl st to form ring. Rnd 1: Ch 1, sc 12 in ring. Rnd 2: Repeat (dc 1, ch 3) around. Rnd 3: Repeat (sc 1, ch 3, dc 5 in dc, sc 1 in 3-ch lp) around. Cut off thread. Make 12 Motif Cs.

Make required number of Motifs D, E, F, and G, following chart. Sew on motifs in slip-stitch (see Diagram for Placement). Put lace cover on Lamp Shade and slip-stitch to shade along sc over foundation ch.

Diagram

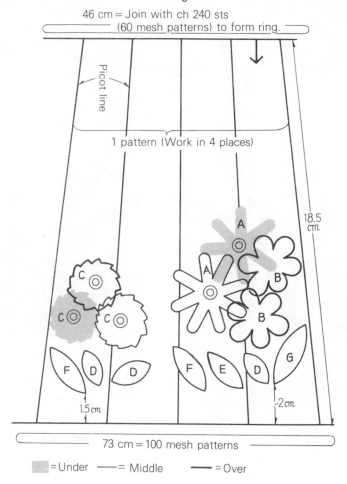

46 cm = Join with ch 240 sts (60 mesh patterns) to form ring.

Picot line

1 pattern (Work in 4 places)

18.5 cm

1.5 cm

~2 cm

73 cm = 100 mesh patterns

■ = Under   — = Middle   — = Over

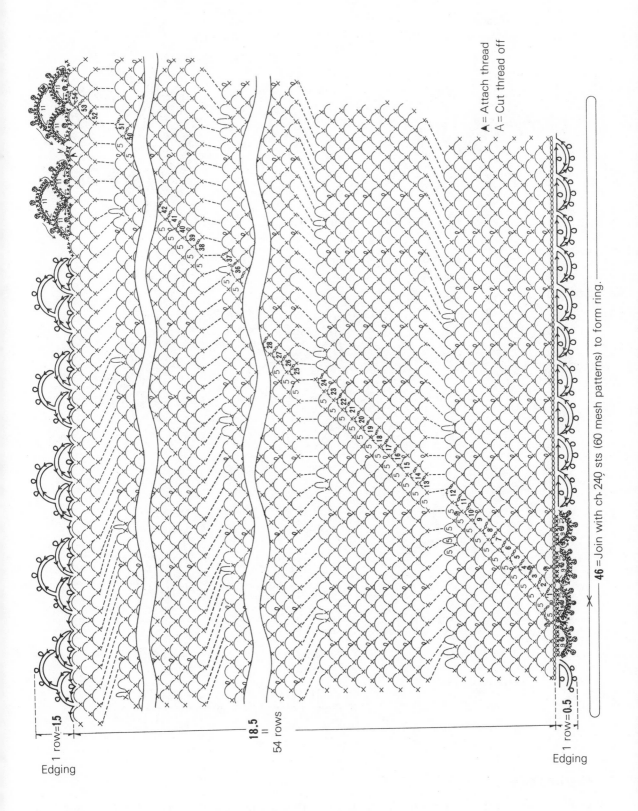

A = Attach thread

A = Cut thread off

46 = Join with ch. 240 sts (60 mesh patterns) to form ring.

Edging

1 row = 1.5

18.5
=
54 rows

1 row = 0.5

Edging

79

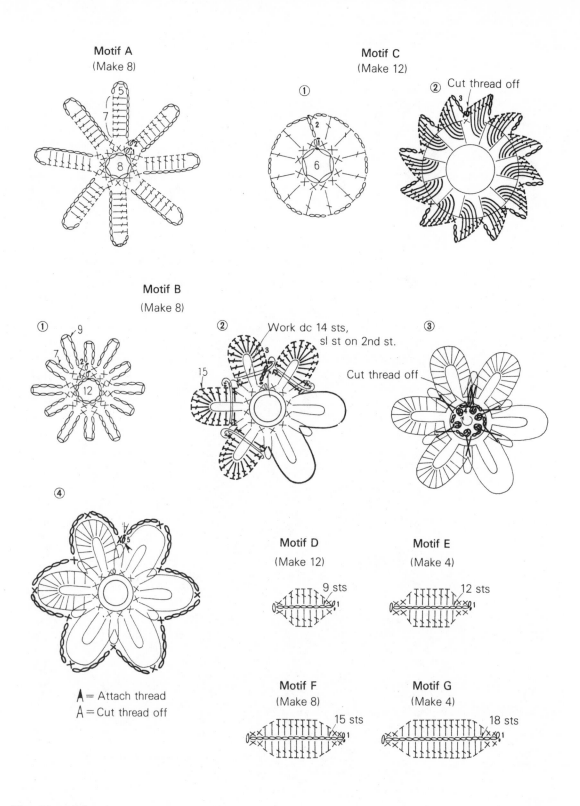

Motif A
(Make 8)

Motif C
(Make 12)

① ② Cut thread off

Motif B
(Make 8)

① ② Work dc 14 sts, sl st on 2nd st. ③ Cut thread off

④

Motif D
(Make 12)

9 sts

Motif E
(Make 4)

12 sts

Motif F
(Make 8)

15 sts

Motif G
(Make 4)

18 sts

A = Attach thread
A = Cut thread off

Matching doily

MATERIALS: Mercerized crochet cotton, No. 40, 10 g beige. Steel crochet hook size 0.90 mm.
FINISHED SIZE: 23 cm in diameter.

DIRECTIONS: Make lp at the end of thread. Rnd 1: Ch 3, dc 1) 7 times, ch 1, hdc 1. Rnds 2–27: Work in mesh pattern, following chart. Increase sts and add picots as indicated.

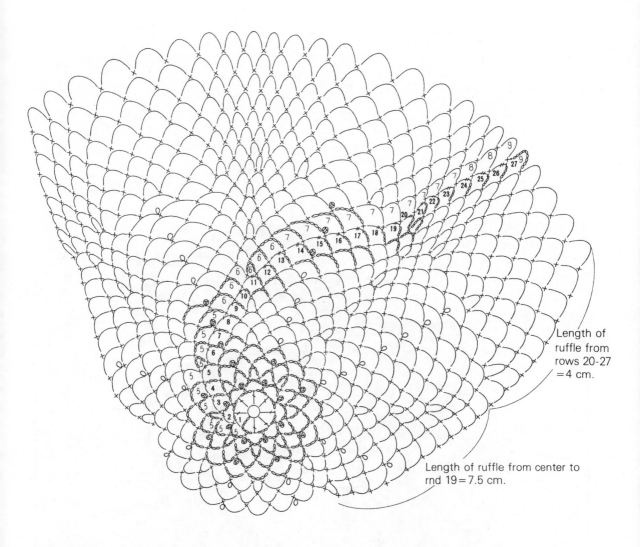

Length of ruffle from rows 20-27 = 4 cm.

Length of ruffle from center to rnd 19 = 7.5 cm.

Window Decoration, *shown on page 29, top.*

MATERIALS: Mercerized crochet cotton, No. 40, 60 g white. Steel crochet hook size 0.90 mm.
FINISHED SIZE: 44.5 cm by 38.5 cm.
GAUGE: 10 cm = 20 bls or sps; 10 cm = 20 rows.
DIRECTIONS: Ch 229. Work 88 rows in filet mesh, following chart. Work 1 rnd of sc for edging.

Edging

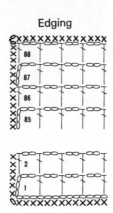

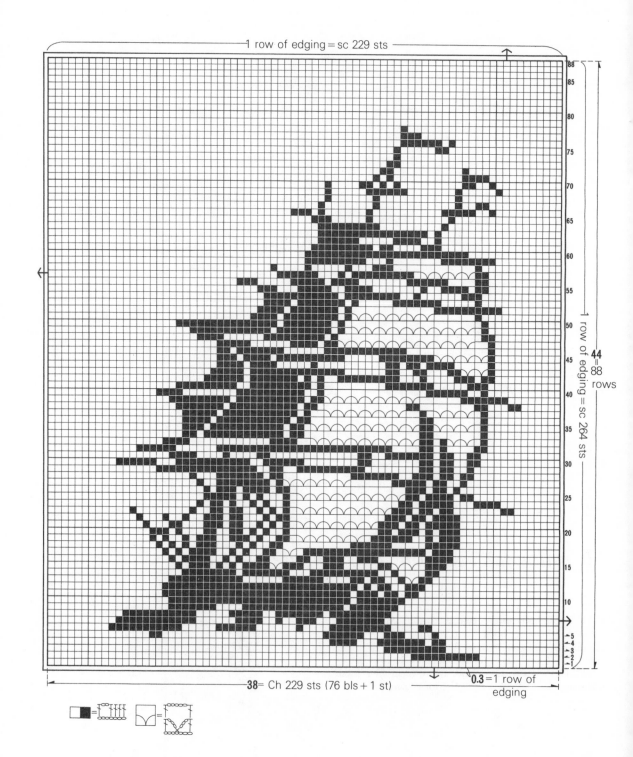

Window Decoration, *shown on page 29,*

bottom.

MATERIALS: Mercerized crochet cotton, No. 40, 60 g
white. Steel crochet hook size 0.90 mm.
FINISHED SIZE: 44.5 cm by 38.5 cm.
GAUGE: 10 cm = 20 bls or sps; 10 cm = 20 rows.
DIRECTIONS: Ch 229. Work 88 rows in filet mesh
following chart. Work 1 rnd of sc for edging.

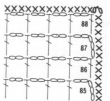

1 row of edging = sc 229 sts

1 row of edging = sc 264 sts

44 = 88 rows

38 = Ch 229 sts (76 bls + 1 st)

0.3 = 1 row of edging

Lace Pictures, *shown on page 34.*

Flower Picture

MATERIALS: Mercerized crochet cotton, No. 40, 5 g
white. Steel crochet hook size 0.90 mm. Navy blue velvet,
20 cm in diameter. Round frame, 13 cm inner diameter
and 20 cm outer diameter. Cardboard, 14 cm in diameter.

FINISHED SIZE: See diagram.

GAUGE: Width of crocheted cord = 0.3 cm.

Motif A: 2.8 cm in diameter; Motif B: 2 cm in diameter.

DIRECTIONS: Make 2 crocheted cords, 52 cm length for
outline of flower, and 36 cm length for outer circle,
following directions on page 96. Join ends of each cord to
form ring. Make 1 Motif A and 6 Motif Bs, following
chart. Attach Motifs A and B onto background fabric in
slip stitch with tiny stitches. Stitch in running st, 9 cm
radius from center. Cut cardboard same size of frame.
Mount and frame.

Diagram (Actual-size)

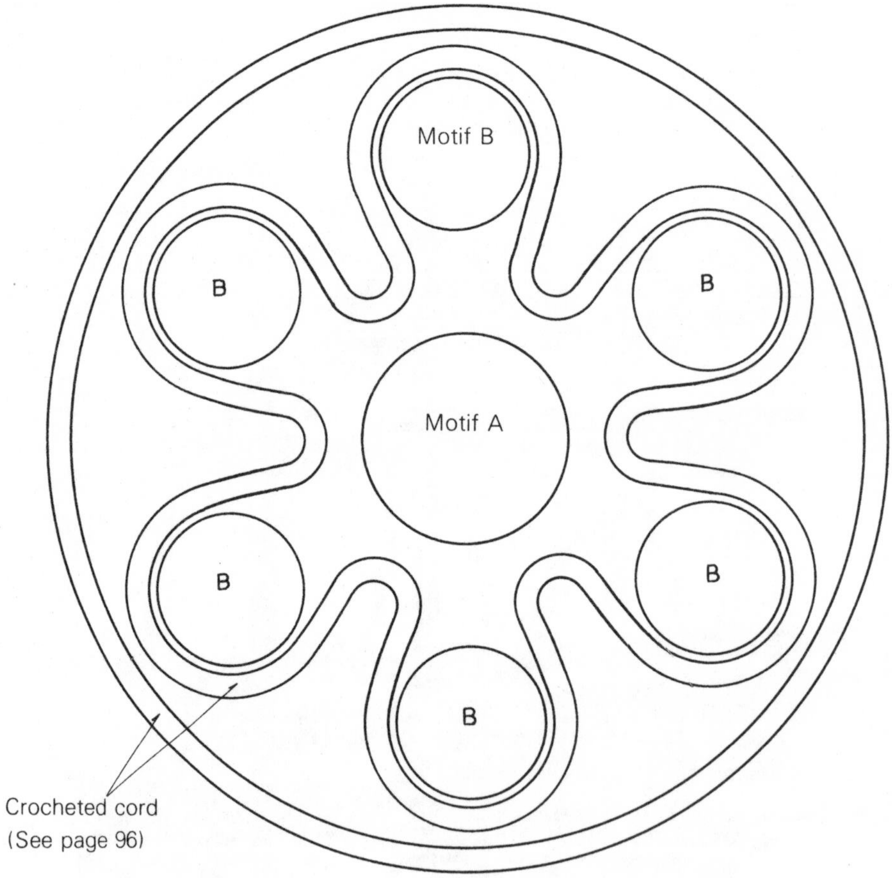

Motif B

B

B

Motif A

B

B

B

Crocheted cord
(See page 96)

Motif A (Make 1)

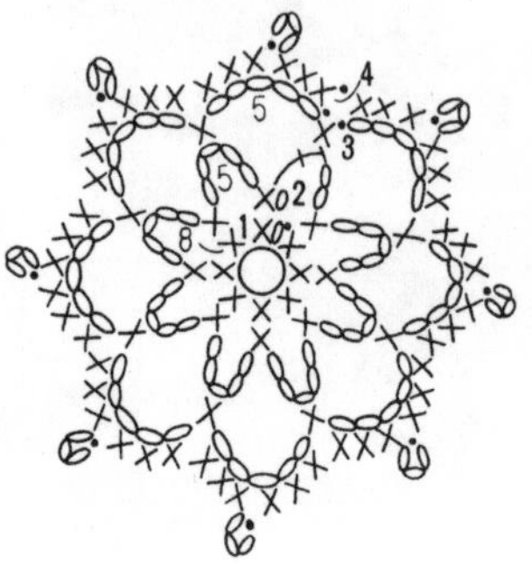

Motif B (Make 6)

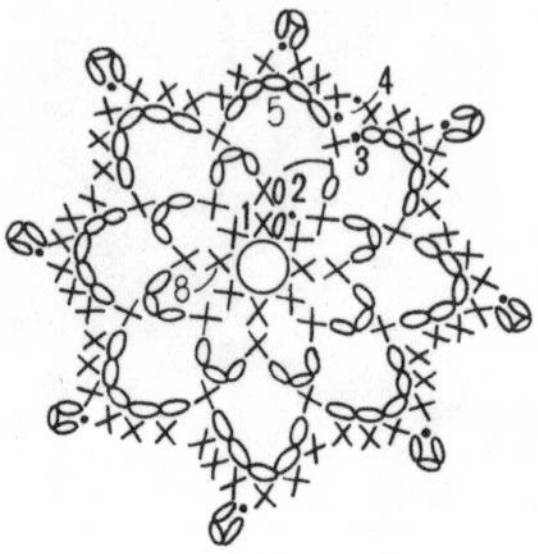

84

Butterfly Picture

MATERIALS: Soft twisted cotton thread [same thickness as pearl cotton # 8]. Mercerized crochet cotton, No. 40, 5 g white. Steel crochet hooks size 1.25 mm and 0.90 mm. Dark wine red velvet, 20 cm in diameter. Round frame, 13 cm inner diameter and 20 cm outer diameter. Cardboard, 14 cm in diameter.
FINISHED SIZE: See diagram.
GAUGE: Width of crocheted cord = 0.5 cm. Motif A: 1 cm in diameter; Motif B: 0.8 cm in diameter; Motif C: 2 cm (length of body).
DIRECTIONS: Make crocheted cord using soft twisted cotton thread and 1.25 mm crochet hook. Use mercerized crochet cotton, No. 40 and 0.90 mm crochet hook for inside of wings and antennae. Make 2 crocheted cords, 21.5 cm each, for outline of wings. For body, make 2 cm crocheted cord, work 1 rnd of sl st around cord, ch 15, end with sl st in 11th st. Cut off thread. Ch 15 for antenna. Make another antenna. Make required number of Motifs A and B, following chart. Make 36 cm crocheted cord for outline, and join ends to form ring. Transfer outline of wings on cardboard and baste crocheted cord onto it. Place Body C between wings, with wrong side up and baste. Place Motifs A and B in same manner and sew Motifs to cord. Fill inside of wings, following directions on next page. After finishing, remove butterfly from cardboard. Sew onto background fabric. Sew on outer circle. Stitch in running st, 9 cm from center. Mount and frame.

How to join ends of crocheted cord

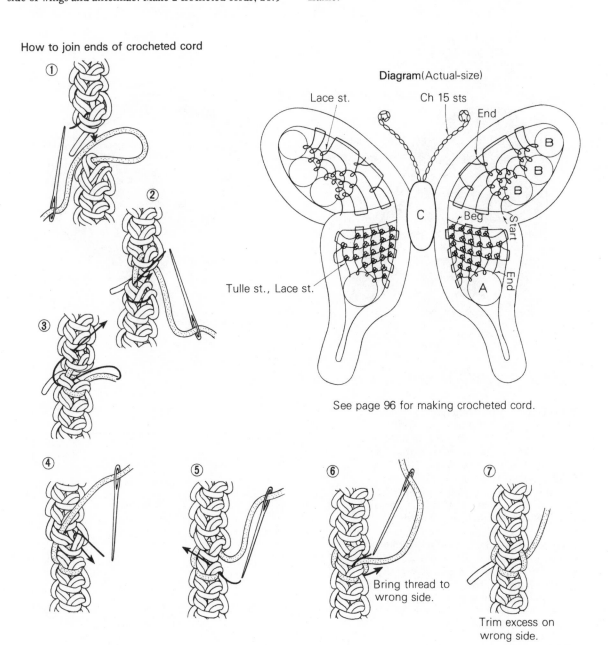

Diagram(Actual-size)

See page 96 for making crocheted cord.

85

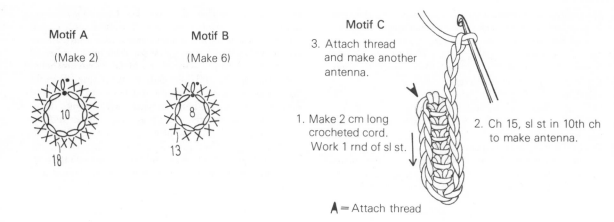

Motif A

(Make 2)

10

18

Motif B

(Make 6)

8

13

Motif C

3. Attach thread and make another antenna.

1. Make 2 cm long crocheted cord. Work 1 rnd of sl st.

2. Ch 15, sl st in 10th ch to make antenna.

A = Attach thread

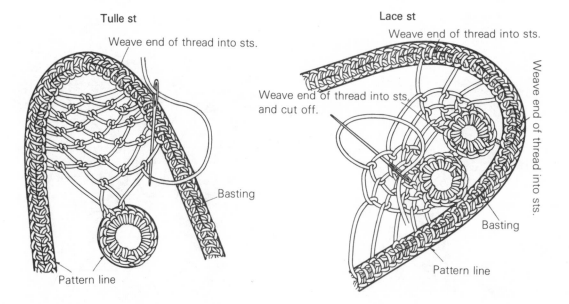

Tulle st

Weave end of thread into sts.

Basting

Pattern line

Lace st

Weave end of thread into sts.

Weave end of thread into sts. and cut off.

Weave end of thread into sts.

Basting

Pattern line

Bedspread, *shown on pages 32 & 33.*

MATERIALS: 3-ply cotton yarn [same thickness as pearl cotton # 3], 2850 g beige. Steel crochet hook size 1.40 mm.
FINISHED SIZE: 245 cm by 165 cm.
SIZE OF MOTIF: 40 cm square.
DIRECTIONS: To make motif, ch 7, join with sl st to form ring. Rnd 1: Ch 3, dc 2, (ch 3, dc 3) 3 times, ch 1, hdc 1. Rnds 2–17: Work following chart. Make design in 5-ch popcorn sts. Make second motif in same manner, but join with sl st to corners and ch of popcorn of first motif on Rnd 17. With wrong sides together, overcast motifs by joining half st of each side. Make and join 24 motifs—4 motifs by 6 motifs. Work for 3 rnds of edging. Work in sc variation on Rnd 3. End off.

Diagram

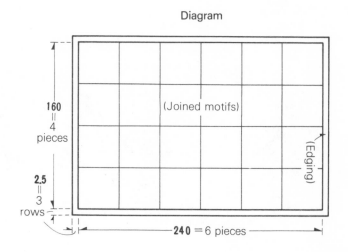

160
=
4
pieces

(Joined motifs)

(Edging)

2.5
=
3
rows

240 = 6 pieces

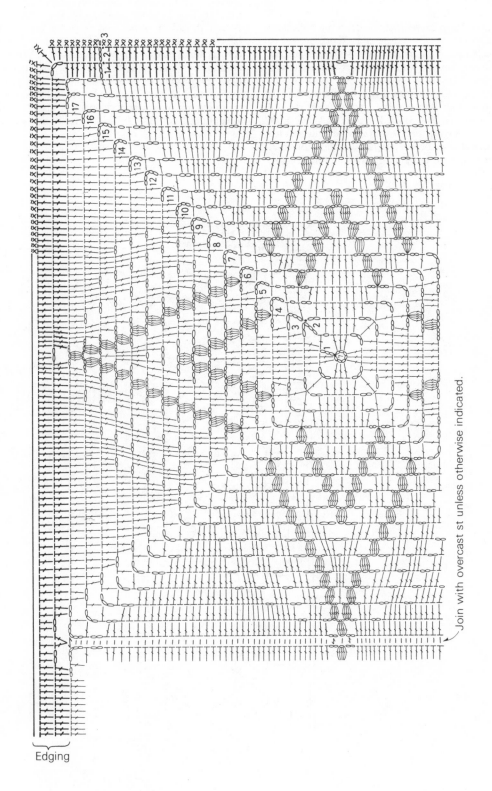

Join with overcast st unless otherwise indicated.

Edging

87

Doily, *shown on page 35.*

MATERIALS: Mercerized crochet cotton, No. 40, 35 g white. Steel crochet hook size 0.90 mm.

FINISHED SIZE: 37 cm by 25 cm.

GAUGE: 1 dc = 0.6 cm.

DIRECTIONS: Make Leaves first. Ch 21. Sc on both sides of foundation ch. Sc 5 in ch at end. Work 9 rows in ribbed st, adding 2 more sts at corner. Make second Leaf in same manner, but join with sl st to first Leaf on Row 9. Make and join 4 Leaves.

Make Flowers. Ch 8. Join with sl st to form ring. Rnd 1: Ch 1, sc 16 in ring. Rnd 2: Ch 1, repeat (sc 1, ch 3) 8 times, end with sl st. Rnd 3: Ch 1, repeat (sc 1, hdc 1, dc 2, hdc 1, sc 1) in 3-ch lp, end with sl st. Rnd 4: Repeat (ch 4, sl st in back of work between petals) around. Rnds 5-7: Work as for Rnds 3-4, but join to Leaves on Rnd 7. Make and join 4 Flowers.

Attach thread and work 2 rnds for edging. Rnd 1: Work in ch, tr, dc and sc joining motifs. Rnd 2: Work in sc all around. Cut off thread. Make one more square in same manner. Join 2 squares, overcasting at center.

Attach thread at corner and work for border. Rnd 1: Work in dc all around, but work (dc 3, ch 3, dc 3) in sc at corners and 2 dc together at center. Rnd 2: Work in sc all around, but work (sc 1, ch 2, sc 1) in 3-ch lp at corners. Rnds 3-7: Work in mesh pattern with 3-ch picots, end with 2 ch, 3-ch picot, 3 ch and tr. Rnd 8: Work in tr and ch all around, end with 5 ch and dtr. Rnd 9: Work in sc all around. Rnds 10-11: Work as for Rnds 1-2. End off.

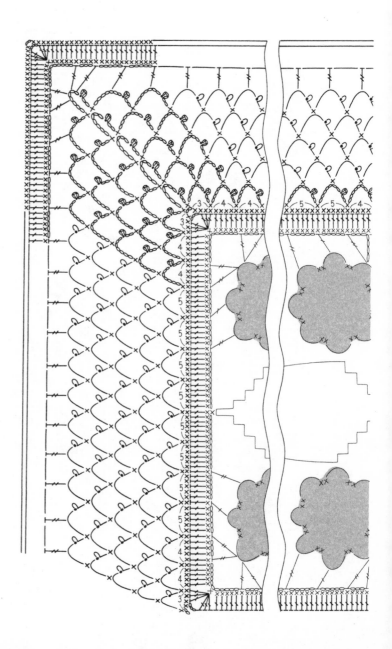

Flower motif

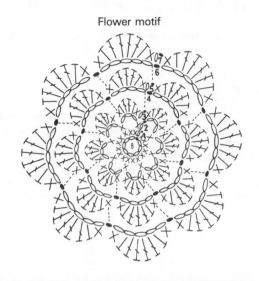

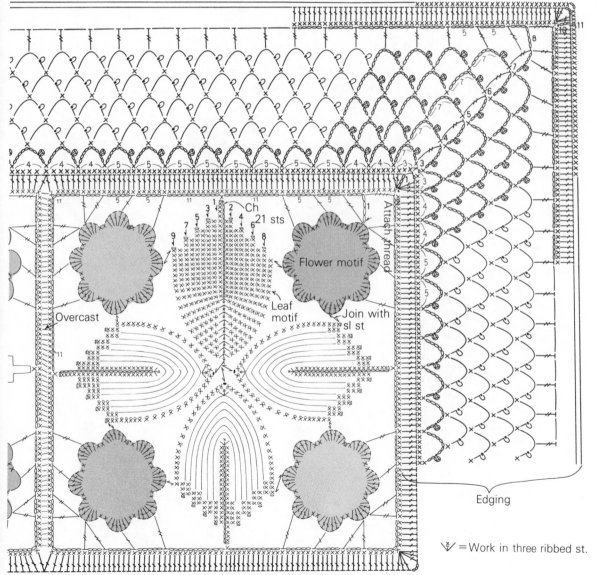

Overcast

Flower motif

Leaf motif

Join with sl st

Attach thread

Ch 21 sts

Edging

$\vee\!\!\!\!\!\times$ = Work in three ribbed st.

89

Tray Mat, *shown on page 36.*

MATERIALS: Mercerized crochet cotton, No. 40, 15 g white. Steel crochet hook size 0.90 mm. White linen, 28.5 cm by 23 cm.

FINISHED SIZE: 36.5 cm by 31 cm.

GAUGE: 1 dc = 0.5 cm.

SIZE OF MOTIF: 5.5 cm by 4.5 cm.

DIRECTIONS: Fold all sides of white linen, turning 0.3 cm from edge twice. Sc all around over hem, working 5 sc at corners.

How to Make Motifs: Make lp at the end of thread. Rnd 1: Sc 1, ch 21, sc 1, ch 25, sc 1, ch 29, sc 1, ch 25, sc 1, ch 5, end with sl st. Rnd 2: Work following chart. Join tops of 3 petals to sc of white linen with sl st. Make and join 18 Flowers.

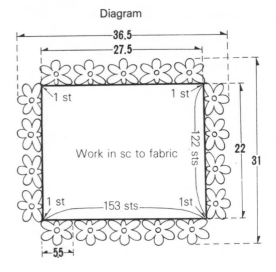

Diagram

Work in sc to fabric

Making motifs and Joinning

$\underline{x\underline{I}}$ =Work stitch scooping 2 ch

Foundation fabric

$\underline{t\vee}$ Work in 5 sc

90

Butterfly Tablecloth, *shown on page 37.*

MATERIALS: Soft twisted cotton thread [same thickness as pear 1 cotton # 8], 240 g white. Steel crochet hook size 1.25 mm.

FINISHED SIZE: 110 cm in diameter.

GAUGE: 1 dc = 0.9 cm.

DIRECTIONS: Work in numerical order from 1 to 8.

1. Ch 7. Repeat (ch 7, dc 7 in ch, ch 5, dc 7) to make braid. After finishing Row 96, join ends following directions on page 98. Cut off thread.

2. Ch 8. Join with sl st to form ring. Rnd 1: Ch 3, dc 23 in ring, end with sl st. Rnds 2–3: Work following chart. Rnd 4: Repeat (sc 1, ch 29, sl st in 5-ch lp of braid, ch 2, dc 27 in each ch) 24 times. Cut off thread.

3. Ch 8. Join with sl st to form ring. Rnd 1: Ch 3, dc 23 in ring, end with sl st. Rnds 2–5: Work in dc and ch to make lower wing. Rnd 6: Work in hdc, ch, dc, tr and dtr. Cut off thread. Make one more lower wing in same manner, reversing pattern. Work 1 row of edging around wings, joining to 7-ch lp of braid with septuple dc.

4. Attach thread at dc of Rnd 1 of lower wing. Make upper wings in same manner as for lower wings. work 1 rnd of edging around wings, overlapping 3-ch lps of upper and lower wings. Join to adjacent butterfly with septuple dc.

5. Make body. Ch 4. Join with sl st to form ring. Rnd 1: Ch 3, dc 9 in ring. Rnds 2–6: Work in dc to make tube. Rnd 7: Repeat (dc 2, 2-dc cluster) to decrease to 8 sts. Rnd 8: Repeat (sc 4, ch 17, dtr 1 in lp of upper wing, sc 17) twice.

6. Make braid for outer circle in same manner as for 1. Work 256 rows.

7. Rnd 1: Repeat (dtr 2, ch 9) around. Rnds 2–30: Work following chart. Increase number of ch as you work.

8. Work over dc of 2, repeating (sc 1, 3-ch picot) around. End off.

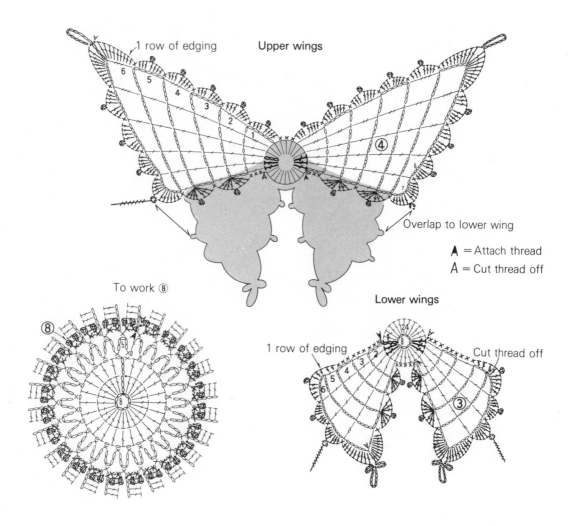

1 row of edging   Upper wings

④

Overlap to lower wing

A = Attach thread

A = Cut thread off

To work ⑧

⑧

Lower wings

1 row of edging   Cut thread off

③

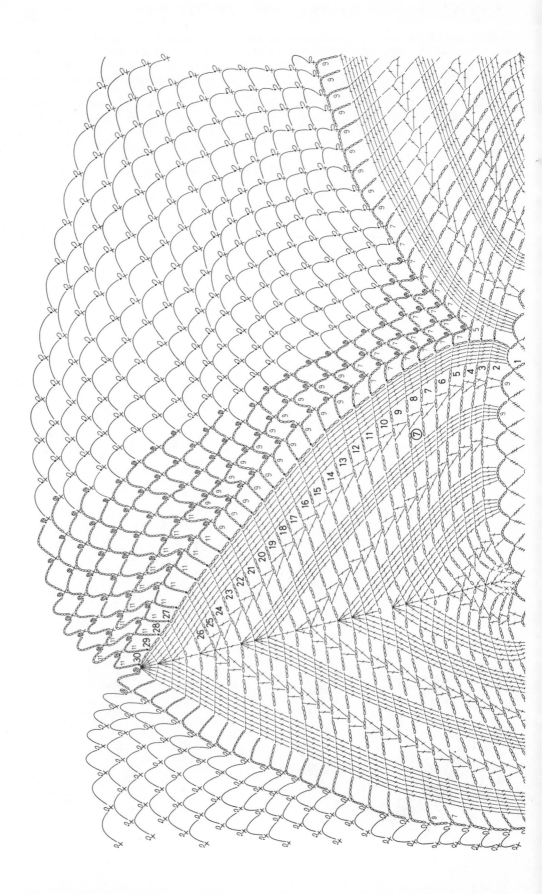

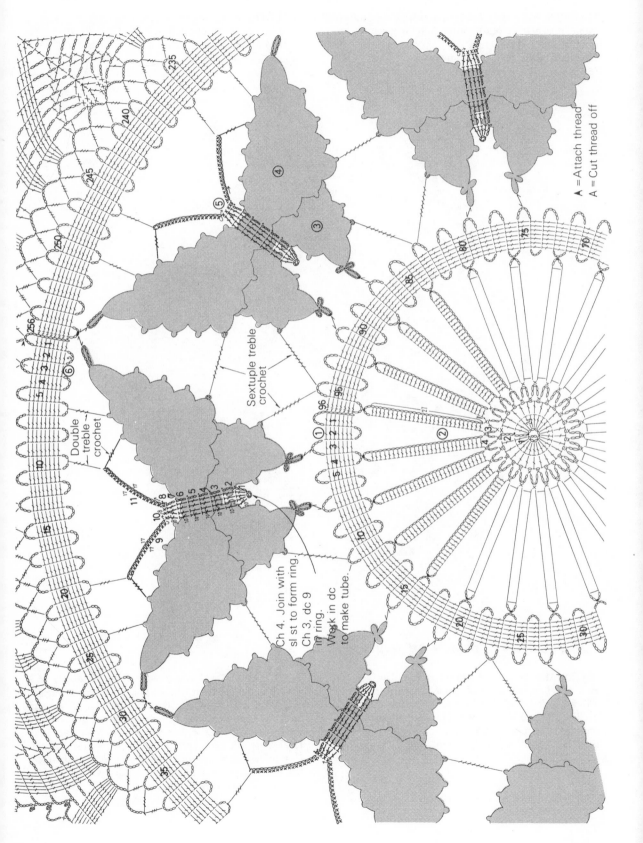

Sextuple treble crochet

Double treble crochet

Ch 4. Join with sl st to form ring.
Ch 3, dc 9 in ring.
Work in dc to make tube.

A = Attach thread
A = Cut thread off

Flower Coasters, *shown on page 38.*

MATERIALS: (for one coaster): Soft twisted cotton thread [same thickness as pearl cotton # 8], 6 g white. Steel crochet hook size 1.00 mm.
FINISHED SIZE: 12.5 cm in diameter.
GAUGE: 1 dc = 0.7 cm.

DIRECTIONS: Ch 6. Join with sl st to form ring. Rnd 1: Ch 1, sc 12 in ring, end with sl st. Rnd 2: Ch 4, repeat (ch 5, tr 1) 5 times, ch 5, end with sl st. Rnds 3-11: Work following chart. End off.

Placemats, *shown on page 39.*

MATERIALS: Mercerized crochet cotton, No. 40, 10 g each of white, salmon pink, blue, grayish brown, and mustard. Steel crochet hook size 1.00 mm. Cross-stitch needle. Linen in white, pink, blue, grayish brown, and mustard, 37 cm by 27 cm each.
FINISHED SIZE: 36 cm by 26 cm.

DIRECTIONS: Draw one thread each horizontally and vertically, 0.3 cm from edge of linen. Fold from thread-drawn line and press. Fold 0.3 cm from edge of bias-cut corner and press. Sc over hems working 3 sc at corners. For Flower Motif: Ch 6. Join with sl st to form ring. Rnd 1: Ch 1, repeat (sc 1, ch 5) 6 times, end with sl st. Rnds 2 – 4: Work following chart. Make 55 cm crocheted cord (see page 96) and join ends to form ring. Work in sl st on one side. Attach Flower Motif as shown in pattern.

Diagram

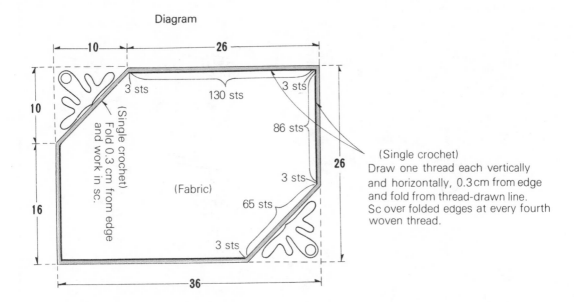

- 10
- 26
- 3 sts
- 130 sts
- 3 sts
- 86 sts
- 10
- 16
- (Single crochet) Fold 0.3 cm from edge and work in sc.
- (Fabric)
- 65 sts
- 3 sts
- 26
- 3 sts
- 36

(Single crochet)
Draw one thread each vertically and horizontally, 0.3 cm from edge and fold from thread-drawn line. Sc over folded edges at every fourth woven thread.

Flower motif

Actual-size Pattern

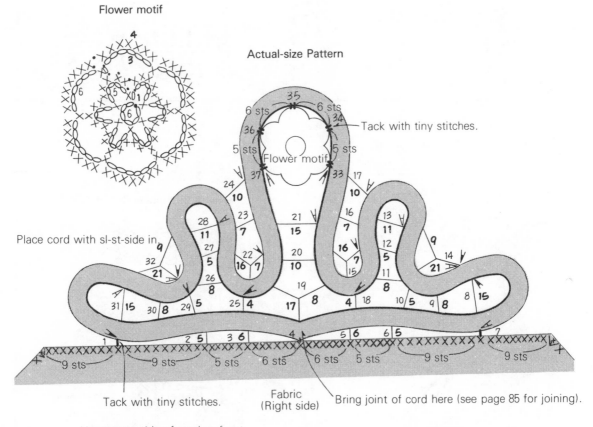

Tack with tiny stitches.

6 sts 6 sts

5 sts 5 sts

Flower motif

Place cord with sl-st-side in.

Tack with tiny stitches.

Fabric (Right side)

Bring joint of cord here (see page 85 for joining).

9 sts 9 sts 5 sts 6 sts 6 sts 5 sts 9 sts 9 sts

Use wrong side of cord as front.

Boldface numbers indicate number of buttonhole stitches required.

Other numbers indicate sequence of buttonholing.

⋏ marks beginning and ⋏ ending.

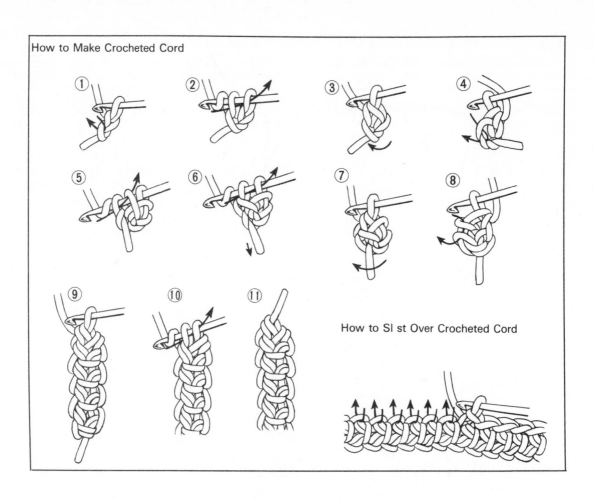

How to Make Crocheted Cord

① ② ③ ④

⑤ ⑥ ⑦ ⑧

⑨ ⑩ ⑪

How to Sl st Over Crocheted Cord

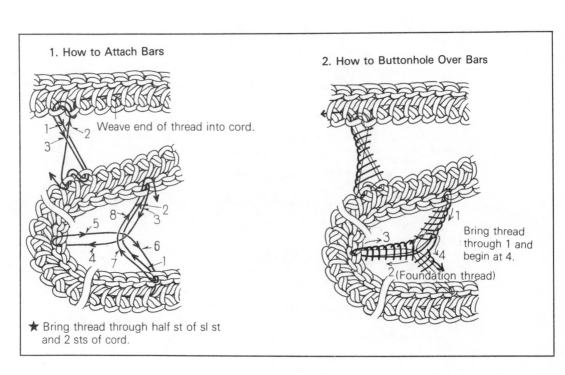

1. How to Attach Bars

Weave end of thread into cord.

1
2
3

8
5   2
       3

4   7   6

       1

★ Bring thread through half st of sl st and 2 sts of cord.

2. How to Buttonhole Over Bars

1

3
       4
2 (Foundation thread)

Bring thread through 1 and begin at 4.

96

Mats, *shown on page 40.*

MATERIALS: Mercerized crochet cotton, No. 18, 20 g white for Large Mat and 15 g for Small Mat. Steel crochet hook size 1.50 mm.
FINISHED SIZE: Large Mat: 20 cm in diameter; Small Mat: 16 cm in diameter.
GAUGE: 1 dc = 1 cm.

DIRECTIONS: For Large Mat: Ch 12. Join with sl st to form ring. Rnd 1: Ch 1, sc 16 in ring. Rnd 2: Ch 3, repeat (ch 2, dc 2) 15 times, ch 2, end with sl st. Rnd 3: Ch 1, sc all around. Rnd 4: Ch 14, ch 1, sc in each ch, dc 1, sl st in sc on Rnd 3, sl st in next sc, turn, sc 14, turn, sc 14, end with sl st. Make 7 more petals in same manner. Rnd 5: Work in sc over double strands of 110 cm foundation thread, forming lps as shown. Join to top of petals with sl st. Rnd 6: Work in sc over double strands of 130 cm foundation thread in same manner as for Rnd 5, end with sl st in sc of Rnd 5.
For Small Mat: Make as for Large Mat up to Rnd 5.

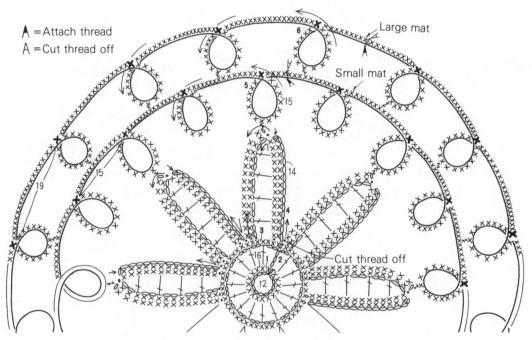

 = Attach thread
 = Cut thread off

X = Work sc over crossed foundation thread to form ring.

XXX = Work in sc over double strands of foundation thread.

THE BASICS IN CROCHETING

TO BEGIN

A: Begin with ch to form ring.

B: Begin with lp.

  ① ②  ③  ④ ⑤

After working
required sts,
draw end of lp.

TO JOIN ENDS OF BRAID

①

On last row, ch 5.
Drop lp from hook.
Pull first ch of foun-
dation ch. Insert
hook in 2 lps and pull
dropped lp through
lps.

②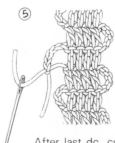

Dc in last dc on last
row.

③

Drop lp from hook.
Pull dropped lp
through lps as in (1).

④

Repeat step (1) 3
times. Dc in first dc
on last row.

⑤

After last dc, cut off
thread. Pull thread
through first ch and
thread needle. Sew
end of ch onto braid
and weave in end of
thread.

HOW TO INC OR DEC IN FILET CROCHET

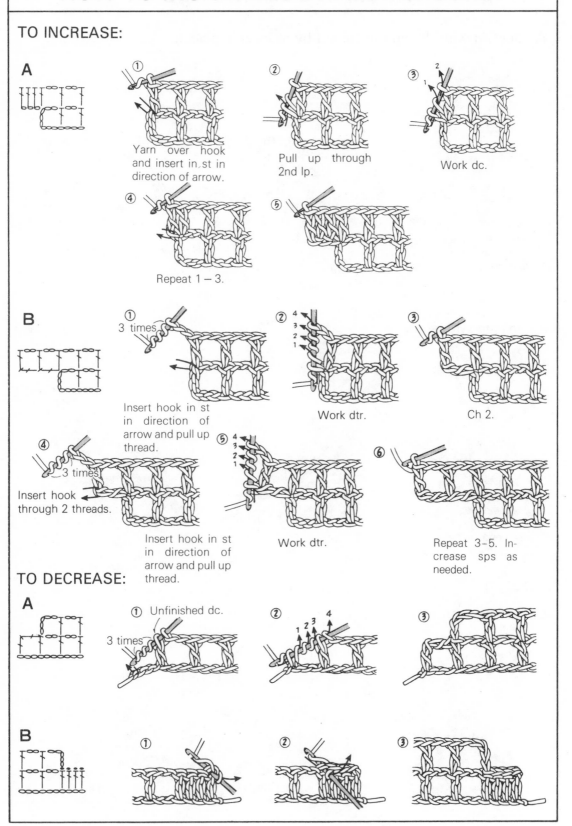

TO INCREASE:

A

① Yarn over hook and insert in st in direction of arrow.

② Pull up through 2nd lp.

③ Work dc.

④

⑤ Repeat 1 – 3.

B

① 3 times
Insert hook in st in direction of arrow and pull up thread.

② Work dtr.

③ Ch 2.

④ 3 times
Insert hook through 2 threads.
Insert hook in st in direction of arrow and pull up thread.

⑤ Work dtr.

⑥ Repeat 3–5. Increase sps as needed.

TO DECREASE:

A

① Unfinished dc.
3 times

②

③

B

①

②

③

HOW TO JOIN MOTIFS

A: Joining with drawn-out thread by re-inserting hook.

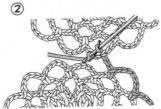

①

Drop lp from hook. Insert hook in sp of net, pick up dropped lp, and pull up through net.

②

Continue working in ch.

③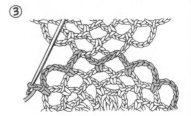

B: Joining with sl st.

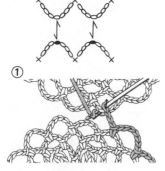

①

Insert hook in net.
Pull up thread through net.

②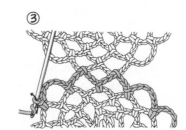

③

C: Joining with sc.

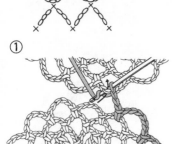

①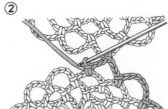

②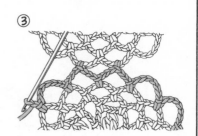

③

BASIC CROCHET STITCHES

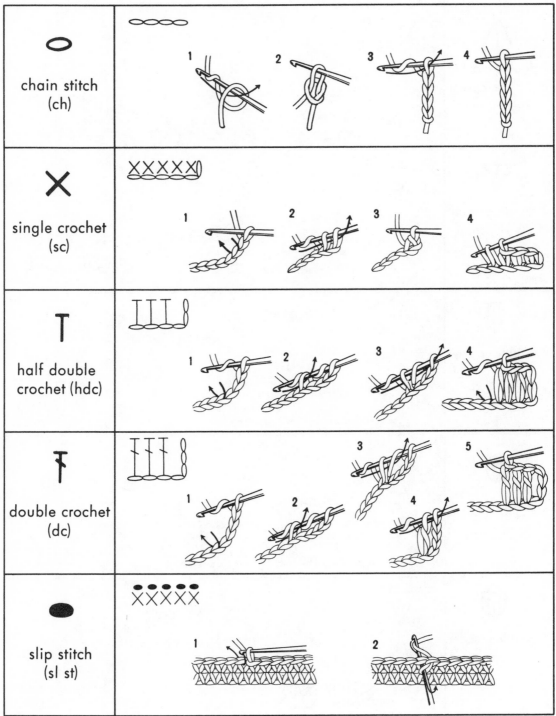

chain stitch (ch)	1 2 3 4
single crochet (sc)	1 2 3 4
half double crochet (hdc)	1 2 3 4
double crochet (dc)	1 2 3 4 5
slip stitch (sl st)	1 2

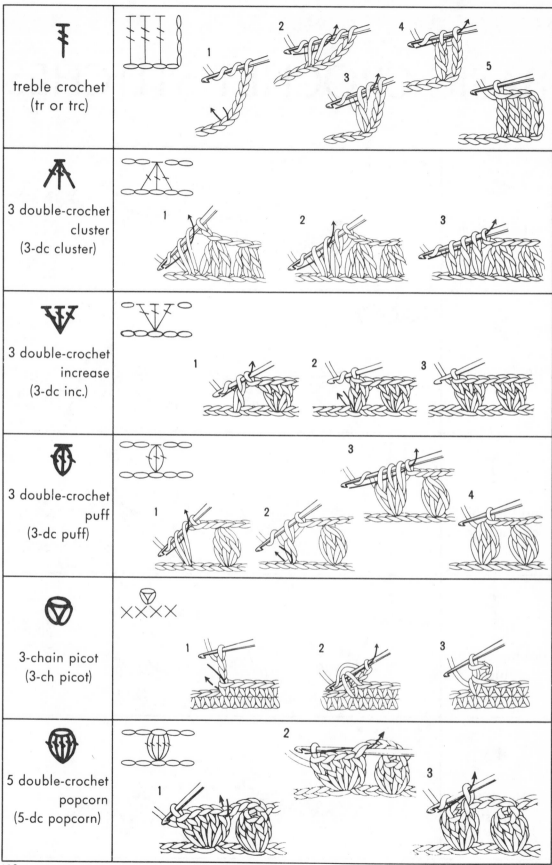

treble crochet (tr or trc)	
3 double-crochet cluster (3-dc cluster)	
3 double-crochet increase (3-dc inc.)	
3 double-crochet puff (3-dc puff)	
3-chain picot (3-ch picot)	
5 double-crochet popcorn (5-dc popcorn)	

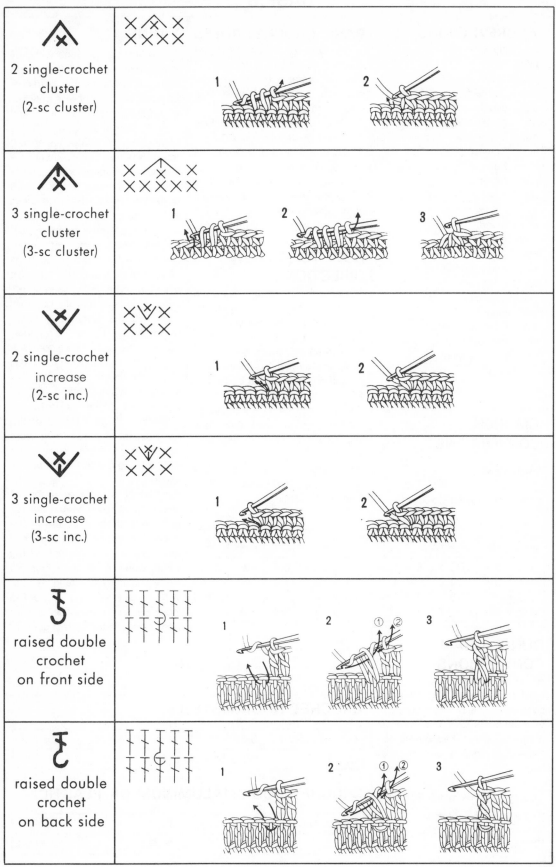

2 single-crochet cluster (2-sc cluster)	
3 single-crochet cluster (3-sc cluster)	
2 single-crochet increase (2-sc inc.)	
3 single-crochet increase (3-sc inc.)	
raised double crochet on front side	
raised double crochet on back side	

BASICS

ABBREVIATIONS

bl	block
beg	begin
ch	chain
dec	decrease
dc	double crochet
dtr	double treble crochet
hdc	half double crochet
inc	increase
No.	Number
patt	pattern
rep	repeat
rs	right side
rnd	round
sl st	slip stitch
sp	space
sc	single crochet
st	stitch
sts	stitches
lp	loop
tr tr	triple treble crochet
yo	yarn over hook
tr	treble crochet
sk	skip

CM/INCH CONVERSIONS

1 inch = 2.54 cm = $\frac{1}{12}$ foot

1 foot = approximately 30 cm

= 12 inchs

inch	cm	inch	cm	inch	cm	inch	cm	inch	cm
1/8	0.3	5/8	1.5	1 1/4	3.2	2 1/2	6.5	8	20.5
1/4	0.6	3/4	2	1 1/2	3.8	3	7.5	10	25.5
3/8	1	7/8	2.2	1 3/4	4.5	4	10	15	38
1/2	1.3	1	2.5	2	5	5	12.5	20	51

OUNCE/GRAM CONVERSIONS

As an aid in interchanging yarns, we have perpared the following conversion chart. It lists common yarn amounts and their ounce/gram equivalents. Please note that these conversions are approximate.

1 ounce = approximately 28 grams

40 grams = 1 1/3 ounces
50 grams = 1 1/4 ounces
100 grams = 3 1/2 ounces

BASIC CROCHET RULES

1. The chain on the hook is never counted as part of a foundation row. For example, if directions say chain 18, You should have 18 in addition to one on the hook.
2. Always insert hook into a chain or stitch from front to back.*
3. Always insert hook under the two top loops of a chain or stitch.*
4. There should be just one loop left on the hook at completion of a stitch or sequence.
*Unless directions say otherwise.

HOW TO FOLLOW DIRECTIONS

The asterisk (*) is used in directions to mark the beginning and end of any part that is to be repeated.
For example "* ch 9, dc 3, repeat from* 4 times" means to work directions after first * until second * is reached, then go back to first * 4 times more, 5 times in all.
When parentheses ( ) are used to show repetition, work directions in parentheses as many times as specified.
For example, "(ch 9, dc 3) 4 times" means to do what is in ( ) 4 times altogether.

YARNS

Crocheting can be done with any stringy material from finest tatting cotton to raffia, leather cords, or fabric strips. Your choice only has to suit the purpose and be worked with an appropriate hook.

Most cotton yarns are mercerized; this means they have undergone a process that strengthens and gives them greater luster. Some also are boilfast, a term that signifies colors will not run or fade in hot water.

If applicable, these terms appear on the label, along with other descriptive information, such as number of plies or cords that have been twisted together, and sometimes a number (usually between 10 and 70) that signifies thickness of the ply. The higher the number, the finer the yarn. If yarn comes in a skein, it is best to wind it in a ball to prevent its tangling in use.

Whatever type of thread you decide to use, be certain to buy at one time sufficient thread of the same dye lot to complete the work you wish to make. It is often impossible to match shades later as dye lots vary.

For perfect results the number of stitches and rows should correspond with those indicated in the directions. Before starting your work, make a small sample of the stitch, working with the suggested hook and desired thread. If your working tension is too tight or too loose, use a coarser or finer crochet hook to obtain the correct gauge.

CROCHET HOOKS (STEEL)

Continental-mm.	0.6	0.75	1	1.25	1.5	1.75	2	2.5	3
U.S.A.	12	10	9	8	7	6	4	2	1

CROCHET HOOKS (ALUMINUM OR PLASTIC)

Continental-mm.	2.5	3	3.5	4	4.5	5	5.5	6	7
U.S.A.	1/B	2/C	4/E	5/F	6/G	8/H	9/I	10/J	10.5/k

We have referred to McCall's "Needlework & Crafts" and Reader's Digest's "Complete Guide to Needlework" for this page's descriptions.